LEAVING CERTIFICATE

LESS STRESS MORE SUCCESS

Biology Revision

Philip Murphy

g GILL EDUCATION

Gill Education
Hume Avenue
Park West
Dublin 12
www.gilleducation.ie

Gill Education is an imprint of M. H. Gill & Co.

978 0 7171 7932 9

Design by Liz White Designs
Artwork and print origination by MPS Limited, a Macmillan Company

At the time of going to press, all web addresses were active and contained information
relevant to the topics in this book. Gill Education does not, however, accept
responsibility for the content or views contained on these websites. Content, views and
addresses may change beyond the publisher or author's control. Students should always
be supervised when reviewing websites.

Image © Alamy: p.131

The author and publisher have made every effort to trace all copyright holders, but
if any has been inadvertently overlooked we would be pleased to make the necessary
arrangement at the first opportunity.

The paper used in this book is made from the wood pulp of managed forests.
For every tree felled, at least one tree is planted, thereby renewing natural resources.

CONTENTS

Introduction

Leaving Certificate Biology is a long and detailed course with a significant amount of Practical work. This Revision Book provides shortened, specific and detailed information, suitable for both Higher level and Ordinary level.

- Each Section begins with a detailed **Check List** of what is required to be known at Higher and Ordinary Level.
- **Sample Leaving Cert questions and marking schemes** are provided at the end of each section.
- **Laboratory Practicals** are described in detail and reasons for particular steps provided where required.
- Expected results of Laboratory Practicals are provided where possible.
- A comprehensive **Glossary** of Leaving Cert **Biology terms and definitions,** with page references, is provided. This covers the full syllabus and will help students define and understand key terms throughout.

 Note: Material that is to be studied only by those taking Higher Level is indicated in the text.

Biology syllabus

The new Biology Syllabus is divided into three units consisting of the following sections:

Unit 1 – Biology: the study of life

1.1 The Scientific Method
1.2 The Characteristics of Life
1.3 Nutrition
1.4 General Principles of Ecology
1.5 Study of an Ecosystem Guidelines

Mandatory activities in unit 1 are:

1. Qualitative food tests for:
   (a) Protein
   (b) Reducing sugar
   (c) Starch
   (d) Lipids
2. Habitat study of a selected ecosystem

Unit 2 – The cell

2.1 Cell Structure
2.2 Cell Metabolism
2.3 Cell Continuity
2.4 Cell Diversity – Tissue, Organs and Systems
2.5 Genetics

Mandatory activities in unit 2 are:

1. Conduct any activity to demonstrate osmosis
2. Use of the light microscope
3. Preparation and examination of animal and plant cells
4. Investigation of the effect of pH on enzyme activity
5. Investigation of the effect of temperature on enzyme activity
6. Investigate the effect of heat denaturation on catalase activity
7. Prepare an enzyme immobilisation and examine its application
8. Investigate the influence of light intensity **or** carbon dioxide on the rate of photosynthesis
9. Prepare and show the production of alcohol by yeast
10. Isolation of DNA from plant tissue

Unit 3 – The organism

3.1 Diversity of organisms and classification
3.2 Organisation complexity in plants
3.3 Transport and nutrition
3.4 Breathing system and excretion
3.5 Responses to stimuli
3.6 Reproduction and growth

Mandatory activities in unit 3 are:

1. Investigation of the growth of leaf yeast using agar plates and controls
2. Prepare and microscopically examine the transverse section of a dicot stem
3. Dissect, display and identify an ox's or a sheep's heart
4. Investigation of the effect of exercise on the breathing rate **or** pulse of a human
5. Investigation of the effect of the growth regulator IAA on plant tissue
6. Investigation of the effect of water, oxygen and temperature on germination
7. To show the digestive activity during germination using starch agar **or** skimmed milk plates

MANDATORY ACTIVITIES

It is compulsory that all Mandatory Activities are carried out in the laboratory, or in the habitat for ecology activities. All records of procedures, results, interpretations, sources of error, safety measures, etc. are to be available for inspection if required.

Breakdown of the Leaving Certificate examination

The examination paper will be presented in three sections, as follows:

Section A
Answer any five questions out of six: (5 × 20 marks)
Two questions from Unit 1.
Two questions from Unit 2.
Two questions from Unit 3.

Section B
Answer any two questions out of three: (2 × 30 marks)

The questions in this section are based on the Mandatory Activities and the manipulation of data.

Section C
Answer any four questions out of six: (4 × 60 marks)
One question from Unit 1.
Two questions from Unit 2.
Three questions from Unit 3.

The summary of the marks awarded for each section of the examination paper is provided below:

Section	Marks	% of Total	Estimated Time in Exam
A	100	25%	30 minutes
B	60	15%	20 minutes
C	240	60%	120 minutes
Total	**400**	**100%**	170 minutes

Total exam time is 180 minutes. It is advised to spend up to 10 minutes reading the entire paper before starting.

UNIT 1

Biology: The Study of Life

Definitions

- Hypothesis
- Theory
- Principle or law
- Variables (fixed/controlled and manipulated)
- Control
- Experiment*
- Data*
- Replicates*
- Fair test*
- Double blind testing*

*defined in the glossary

Outline

- Process of Scientific Method
- Limitations of Scientific Method

In general, a scientist develops a **hypothesis** to explain an observed event.

- The steps of the scientific method are used to support or refute a hypothesis.
- It is essential, for the support of a hypothesis, that these steps can be repeated independently by any other scientist.
- A hypothesis can become a **theory** over time if the same results can be achieved by independent, unbiased experiments carried out by a number of other scientists.
- A theory that has been confirmed repeatedly over a long period and is universally accepted may then become a **principle** or **law**.

Limitations of Scientific Method

1. Interpretation of results is limited by our present knowledge and abilities.
2. Living organisms are rarely predictable and unknown factors can affect outcomes.
3. Scientists often have theories as to the outcomes of experimentation before the experiment is carried out. These can influence their interpretation of results.
4. Scientific theories are tested to see if they can be proven false. Only one confirmed negative result is needed to disprove a theory, even if hundreds of experiments support it.

Experimentation

In any biology experiment, conditions or factors (light intensity or temperature, for example) can be varied. These **factors** are known as **variables**.

During many experiments, when varying one factor, the other variables must be kept constant.

Control

Every experiment needs a **control** to compare results. A control is generally the same apparatus as the experiment but without the factor under test being varied.

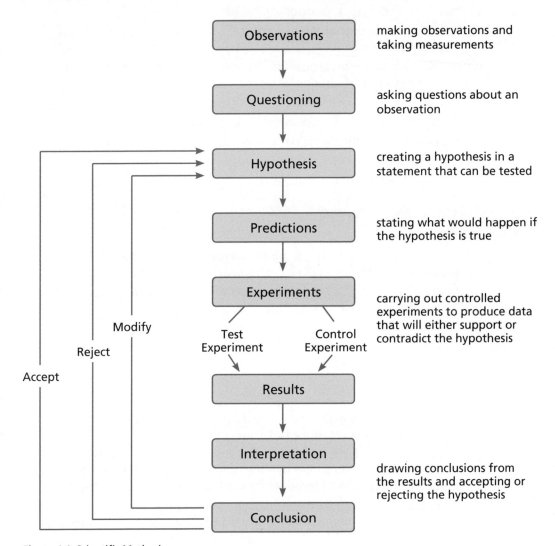

Figure 1.1 Scientific Method

2015 Q9 HIGHER LEVEL

9. (a) (i) What is the purpose of a hypothesis in the scientific method?

    (ii) Explain what is meant by double-blind testing in scientific experimentation.

(b) A scientist wished to investigate the effect of the concentration of iodine on the rate of growth of tadpoles (young frogs). He acquired 100 tadpoles of the same age, all of which had hatched from the fertilised eggs of one female. He used water from the pond in which the tadpoles had hatched, and a stock solution of iodine.

    (i) Why do you think that it was important that all the tadpoles came from the same mother?

    (ii) At the start of the investigation the scientist divided the tadpoles into four groups of 25, one of which was to be the control.

        1. Why is a control essential in scientific experiments?

        2. Suggest why he used 25 tadpoles in each group.

        3. Suggest how this investigation would have been carried out.

    (iii) Suggest **two** factors that the scientist would have kept constant during the investigation.

LEAVING CERT MARKING SCHEME

9. (a) 5 + 1

(a) (i) To form the basis of a prediction **or** to give a starting point for an experiment **or** (to attempt) to explain an observation

    (ii) Neither the experimenter nor the text group knows who gets what (or described)

(b) 9 + 9 + 6(1)

(b) (i) So they are genetically similar or they are likely to respond in the same way (to iodine)

    (ii) 1. To (provide a standard or baseline to) compare with the experiment

        2. A larger sample makes allowance for illness (or death) **or** to make the results more statistically significant

        3. Different concentrations of iodine (solution) / made up using pond water / 25 tadpoles in each (solution) / leave for a time / record changes in tadpoles / (control) no iodine   **Any three**

    (iii) Temperature / amount of food / oxygen concentration / light (exposure) / volume of water / duration of exposure   **Any two**

1.2 The Characteristics of Life

Definition of life

It is difficult to define **life**, but all living things have two features in common:

1. **Metabolism:** They carry out chemical reactions to live.
2. **Reproduction:** All organisms can produce offspring for **continuity**.

Characteristics of living things (organisms)

There are six characteristics common to all living organisms:

1. **Respiration:** The chemical release of energy from food which occurs at a cellular level.
2. **Nutrition:** The means by which an organism obtains its energy to live, and the matter it needs to build its structures.
3. **Excretion:** The removal of the wastes produced in metabolism from the body.
4. **Movement:** Animal movements are obvious, while plant movements are slow, involving only parts of the plant.
5. **Growth:** An increase in size due to an increase in solid matter in the body. There is usually an associated increase in complexity of the organism as it grows.
6. **Reproduction:** The ability to produce new individuals of the same species.

Food

Most types of **food** are in the form of large, complex **biomolecules.**

The six most common elements in food biomolecules are carbon, hydrogen, nitrogen, oxygen, phosphorus and sulfur. There are four main types of food biomolecules:

1. **Carbohydrates**
2. **Lipids**
3. **Protein**
4. **Vitamins**

Food is any substance used by living organisms to provide energy, materials for repair and maintenance or to control metabolism.

Biomolecules are complex molecules made up of different elements. They are originally produced by plants from simple elements.

Carbohydrates

Carbohydrates contain the elements carbon, hydrogen and oxygen. In general, the ratio of H to O in any carbohydrate is 2:1. The chemical formula for glucose is $C_6H_{12}O_6$.
There are three forms of carbohydrates:

1. Monosaccharides (single units)
2. Disaccharides (double units)
3. Polysaccharides (many units)

Monosaccharides and disaccharides are **soluble** in water.
Sources of monosaccharides and disaccharides are found in foods such as apples, milk and sugar.
Polysaccharides are **insoluble** carbohydrates.
Sources of polysaccharides in food are potatoes, rice and flour.
The main **function** of carbohydrates in the diet is to produce energy.

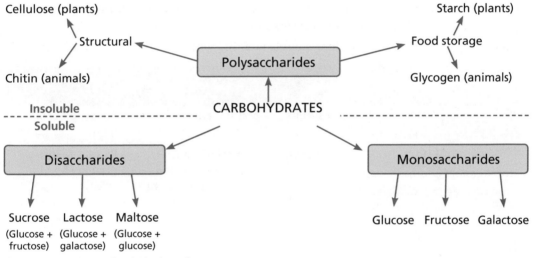

Figure 1.2 Summary of carbohydrate forms

Lipids

Lipids contain the elements carbon, hydrogen and oxygen.
There are two types of lipid:

- **oils,** which are liquid at room temperature
- **fats,** which are solid at room temperature.

The smallest unit of a lipid is called a **triglyceride.** This consists of one molecule of **glycerol** attached to three **fatty acids.**
Sources of lipids are red meats, dairy products and vegetable oils.
Main function in diet: Provide energy and a source of fat-soluble vitamins.

Structural functions: Phospholipids and lipoproteins form cell membranes. Lipids form a protective layer around some body organs, such as the kidneys.

Protein

Protein is made up of the elements carbon, hydrogen, oxygen, nitrogen and occasionally sulfur. The smallest units of proteins are **amino acids**. Most proteins are composed of various proportions of twenty common amino acids.

Main function in the diet: Provide materials for maintenance and repair and provide the building blocks for **enzymes**. Enzymes control chemical reactions in all organisms. Some hormones are made up of protein.

Structural functions: The protein keratin forms hair and nails. The protein myosin forms part of muscle fibres.

Sources of protein include meat, fish, nuts and milk.

Vitamins

Vitamins are **complex organic chemicals** that must be taken in the diet. They are necessary only in **tiny amounts** and often used as coenzymes. Vitamins have no energy value and are classified according to their solubility.

Vitamin C is an example of a water-soluble vitamin, while Vitamin D is fat soluble.

Vitamin	Solubility	Source	Function	Deficiency Disease
C	Water	Citrus fruits	Maintenance of connective tissue	Scurvy, bleeding gums
D	Fat	Fish liver oil, butter	Control of transfer of phosphorus and calcium between the blood and bones	Rickets, failure of growing bones to calcify

Minerals

Minerals are not biomolecules. They are **inorganic chemicals** (simple atoms and ions) necessary in **tiny amounts**. They must be taken in the diet. Minerals have no energy value. Two examples of plant and animal minerals are provided below.

Plant Minerals	Source	Function	Deficiency
Phosphate (PO_4)	Soil	Part of nucleic acids	Poor root growth
Magnesium (Mg)	Soil	Part of chlorophyll	Lack of chlorophyll

Animal Minerals	Source	Function	Deficiency
Iron (Fe)	Liver, meat	Part of haemoglobin and many enzymes	Low red blood cell count
Calcium (Ca)	Milk, cheese	Bones, nerve transmission	Weak bones

Water

Water has no energy value but is essential for life. Over 70 per cent of our body is water. **Water loss** occurs through excretion, breathing and sweating. The average person loses between two and three litres of water per day, which must be replaced in the diet.

Functions of water

- A liquid medium for enzymes to function
- An excellent solvent
- Medium of transport in blood

key point

- Minerals required in relatively large amounts are called **Macronutrients**. These include Sodium (Na), Magnesium (Mg), Chlorine (Cl), Potassium (K) and Calcium (Ca).
- **Trace elements** are minerals required at lower concentrations. Examples are Iron (Fe), Copper (Cu) and Zinc (Zn).

Mandatory activity

Food tests

Test for protein

1. Place a small volume of the sample in a test tube.
2. Add an equal volume of 10 per cent **sodium hydroxide**.
3. Add a few drops of 1 per cent **copper sulfate** and mix.

Positive result = purple OR violet colour.
Negative result = light blue colour.
Control: Use an equal volume of water as the sample.

Test for reducing sugar, e.g. glucose

1. Place a small volume of the sample in a test tube.
2. Add an equal volume of **Benedict's reagent** and mix.
3. Place in a hot water bath for ten minutes (do not boil).

Positive result = brick red OR orange colour. A green colour indicates slight positive result.
Negative result = blue colour.
Control: Use an equal volume of water as the sample.

Test for starch

1. Place a small volume of the sample in a test tube.
2. Add a few drops of dilute **iodine** and mix.

Positive result = blue/black colour.
Negative result = yellow colour.
Control: Use an equal volume of water as the sample.

Test for lipids

1. Heat the sample gently to 40 °C or body temperature.
2. Add the sample to **brown paper**.
3. **Dry** the paper with gentle heat.
4. Hold the paper up to the light.

Positive result = a translucent grease spot is formed.

Negative result = no translucent spot.

Control: Use an equal volume of water as the sample.

2015 Q1 HIGHER LEVEL

1. Answer any **five** of the following parts (a) to (f):
   (a) What name is given to the simplest units of carbohydrates?
   (b) Name a catabolic process that produces these simplest units.
   (c) The general formula of carbohydrates is $C_x(H_2O)_y$.
   What is the most common value of y in the carbohydrates used for energy by human cells?
   (d) Name a structural polysaccharide found in plants.
   (e) Name a polysaccharide, other than the one referred to in part (d), commonly found in plants.
   (f) Which carbohydrate is always found in DNA?

LEAVING CERT MARKING SCHEME

1. 10 + 7 + 3(1) i.e. best five answers from (a) – (f)
   (a) Monosaccharides   (d) Cellulose
   (b) Digestion   (e) Starch
   (c) 6   (f) Deoxyribose

2014 Q2 (b) HIGHER LEVEL

2. (b) (i) How does a phospholipid differ from a fat?
   (ii) Name a fat-soluble vitamin.
   (iii) State a disorder due to a dietary deficiency of the vitamin referred to in (b) (ii).
   (iv) Give any **two** functions of minerals in organisms.

LEAVING CERT MARKING SCHEME

2. 7 + 6 + 7(1)

(b) (i) (A phospholipid) has a phosphate **or** (a phospholipid) has two fatty acids (A fat) has three fatty acids

   (ii) A, D, E **or** K

   (iii) Matching disorder

(iv) Formation of rigid structure (or named) / formation of soft tissue (or named) / formation of fluid (or named) / formation of pigment (or named) / biochemical function of a named mineral / any other specific function(s) of named mineral(s)

1.4 General Principles of Ecology

Definitions

- Ecology
- Ecosystem
- Biosphere
- Habitat
- Niche
- Abiotic factors
- Climatic factors
- Edaphic factors
- Biotic factors
- Food web
- Food chain
- Pyramid of numbers
- Population*
- Community*

*defined in the glossary

Outline

- Energy flow from the sun through plants up food chains
- Construction of food chain and pyramids of numbers
- Limitations of pyramid of numbers
- Pyramid of biomass and its advantages over pyramid of numbers
- Factors that control population numbers (competition, predation, parasitism and symbiosis/mutualism)
- Factors that affect human population (war, famine, contraception and disease)

Practical Activity

- Study of an ecosystem

IMPORTANT DEFINITIONS

Ecology is the scientific study of how organisms interact with each other and their environment.

An **ecosystem** is a definable area containing a self-sustained community of organisms interacting with their non-living environment.

Examples: Pond, woodland or seashore ecosystems.

The **biosphere** is the part of the earth occupied by organisms. It extends from the bottom of the oceans to the upper atmosphere. It is a relatively thin band compared with the total size of the earth and the atmosphere.

A **habitat** is the part of an ecosystem where individual organisms live.

A **niche** describes the role of an organism in an ecosystem. It shows *how* as well as *where* an organism lives.

Example: A caterpillar feeds and lives on the leaves of an oak tree in a woodland. The caterpillar is also a food source for blue tits in this habitat.

Environmental factors in an ecosystem

The **distribution** of organisms in any habitat will be affected by two groups of factors:

- **Abiotic factors**
- **Biotic factors**

Abiotic factors

Abiotic factors are physical, non-living factors that influence living organisms. Abiotic factors include the following:

1. **Climatic factors** such as light, temperature, water availability and wind.
2. **Edaphic factors** (usually associated with soil) such as soil texture, pH and organic content.
3. **Topographic factors** such as the angle or aspect of a slope.

Biotic factors

Biotic factors are any factors in an organism's environment that are due to the presence of other organisms.

Two examples of biotic factors are provided below:

1. The effect of abundant seaweeds on a rocky seashore is to provide shelter and food for a large community of organisms.
2. In a terrestrial (land) ecosystem, biotic factors could include parasitism. Greenfly act as parasites on green plants. They feed on the sap in the phloem, causing harm to the plant.

key point

- On the seashore, abiotic factors would include tides, water temperature and wave action.
- In a woodland ecosystem, abiotic factors would include light, temperature, air humidity, soil pH and wind.

Energy flow in an ecosystem

The **energy** for all living organisms originally comes from the sun.

Food web

A **food web** shows all the feeding (energy change) relationships in an ecosystem (see fig. 1.3).

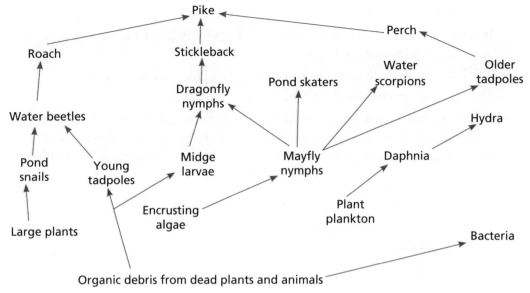

Figure 1.3 Food web (pond)

Food chain

A **food chain** indicates the feeding (energy change) relationships between a number of organisms in an ecosystem.

A food chain from the pond food is shown in fig. 1.4.

Figure 1.4 Food chain

Pyramid of numbers

A **pyramid of numbers** is produced when the number of organisms per unit area is counted at each trophic level in the food chain. The numbers of each organism are then represented by the width of a horizontal bar on the pyramid.

- A food chain or web always begins with a plant (primary producer).
- A food chain or pyramid rarely has more than five stages. This is due to the enormous amounts of energy lost (over 90 per cent) when moving from one trophic level to the next. This energy loss is due to metabolism, excretion, movement or any other living activities.

HL Limitations of a pyramid of numbers

- It can be difficult to count the number of plants (example grasses or algae) accurately in a trophic level.
- There is often more than one organism at any trophic level in a habitat.
- The shape of a pyramid will vary according to the time of year.
- It does not take into account the relative size of the organisms at each level. In a woodland habitat, an example of a food chain and the associated pyramid of numbers is shown in fig. 1.5. This shape is called an inverted pyramid of numbers.

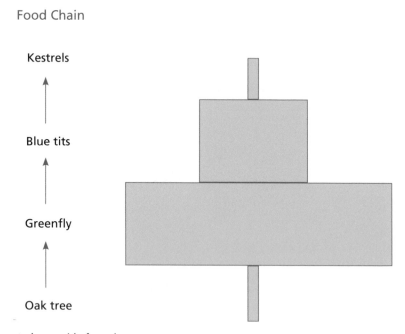

Food Chain

Kestrels

↑

Blue tits

↑

Greenfly

↑

Oak tree

Figure 1.5 Inverted pyramid of numbers

Pyramid of biomass

An alternative approach to a pyramid of numbers is a pyramid of biomass. This is produced by estimating the **dry mass of organisms per unit area** at each level of a food chain (units = kg/m^2). This is regarded as a better procedure because:

- It usually produces the expected pyramid shape due to the inclusion of the factor of organism size into the calculations (see fig. 1.6).
- It can allow for comparisons between ecosystems.

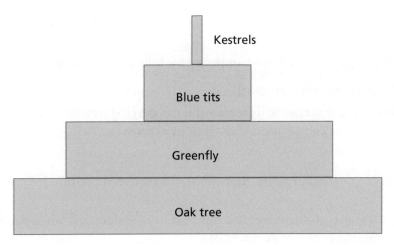

Figure 1.6 Pyramid of biomass

Factors that affect population numbers in an ecosystem

There are four main factors that can influence population numbers in an ecosystem.

1. Competition
2. Predation
3. Parasitism
4. Symbiosis

1. Competition

Competition is usually more intense between members of the same species, due to their requirements for the same resources in the ecosystem.

> **Competition** is the struggle between two or more organisms for limited resources in an ecosystem.

There are two types of competition:

- Contest competition
- Scramble competition

Contest competition involves a physical contest, usually between members of the same species. Only one individual can win the resource.

This form of competition controls population numbers and ensures that only the fittest and strongest reproduce.

Example: Stags compete to reproduce with females in their herd.

Scramble competition involves individuals struggling to get as much of a resource as possible. It usually results in all of the competitors getting some of the resource in the ecosystem.

Scramble competition can lead to a serious decline in competing population numbers if the food source becomes scarce.

Example: Sheep, goats and rabbits competing for hillside vegetation.

Adaptations to avoid competition

The population of any species will increase if it can develop structural or behavioural adaptations to reduce competition with rivals in its ecosystem.

Plants

Plant species can develop different root systems to avoid competition for minerals and water with others.

Example: Grass roots absorb water and minerals from surface soil, while dandelion tap roots source their nutrients from lower layers.

Animals

Animal species can adapt to different food sources in the same ecosystem.

Example: Cormorants and swans both feed in the same estuary ecosystem. Swans are herbivores, feeding on plants. Cormorants are carnivores, feeding on eels and fish.

2. Predation

A **predator** is an organism that feeds on another species, usually killing it first. The other species is called the prey.

The abundance of prey is a factor limiting the numbers of the predator. In a food chain, the predator–prey relationship causes both populations to oscillate (see fig. 1.7).

In this laboratory experiment, the numbers of the predator (paramecium) increase when there is a large population of prey (yeast cells). The increase in predator numbers

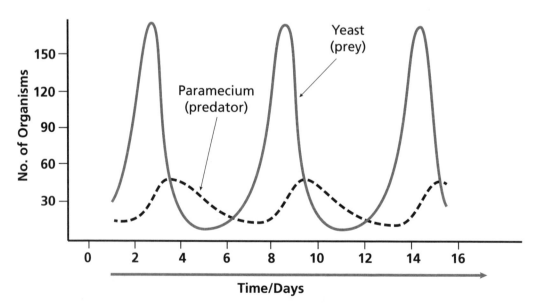

Figure 1.7 Graph of predator–prey relationship

then causes a decrease in the prey population. At this point, predator numbers begin to fall, which allows for prey numbers to increase again.

Population dynamics

In any predator–prey relationship it is likely that factors other than the direct feeding relationship cause variation in the population numbers.

Examples of such factors could include:

- availability of food for the prey
- defence mechanisms developed by the prey
- improvement in techniques of capture by the predator
- competition from other animals in the food web
- the possibility of migration by predator or prey
- the introduction of disease into the predator or prey populations.

Adaptations of predators and prey

Adaptations of predators that improve their efficiency include:

- good vision in hawks to spot prey before being detected
- speed of terriers to capture small mammals
- stealth and agility of cats to capture mice and rats.

Adaptations of prey to avoid capture include:

- camouflage colouration in frogs
- bright colouration of ladybirds warns predators of their unpalatable taste
- snails and slugs will only feed at night to avoid detection.

3. Parasitism

Parasitism is an association where one organism, the parasite, lives in or on another organism, the host. The parasite depends on the host for food and usually causes it harm.

Parasitism can be a limiting factor for the population numbers of the host. This is particularly true when the parasite damages the tissues or causes the early death of the host.

Example: Liverfluke is a parasite in cattle and sheep. Infected animals lose weight and their condition deteriorates.

4. Symbiosis

This is a general term where two different organisms live in close association with one another. One form of **symbiosis** or **mutualism** is where two different organisms live in close association, which provides an advantage to both.

Example: Lichens consist of a fungus and an alga in a mutualistic (symbiotic) relationship. The alga provides food while the fungus provides anchorage and minerals in exchange.

Nutrient recycling

Definitions
• Pollution
• Conservation
• Nutrient recycling*
• Waste management*
*defined in the glossary

Outline
- Stages of carbon cycle
- Stages of nitrogen cycle
- One example of human pollution and its control
- One example of conservation
- Problems associated with waste disposal
- Role of micro-organisms in waste disposal

There is almost a limitless supply of energy provided to the ecosystems by the sun. This is not the situation for nutrients, which must be constantly recycled in nature for the continuity of life.

There are two main **nutrient cycles**:

1. The carbon cycle
2. The nitrogen cycle

The carbon cycle

This describes the changes in the forms of carbon that occur in nature. The cycle is essential for the survival of organisms.

Important points in the carbon cycle include:

- carbon is a basic element of all living things
- all organisms produce carbon dioxide gas as a waste product of respiration
- plants absorb carbon dioxide gas from the air for use in photosynthesis
- photosynthesis produces carbohydrates that can be converted to other foods required by the plant
- animals gain their energy and carbon by feeding directly or indirectly on plants
- combustion of fossil fuels is changing the balance of nature by releasing huge quantities of CO_2 into the air.

Fig. 1.8 shows a summary of the changes in the forms of carbon that occur in nature.

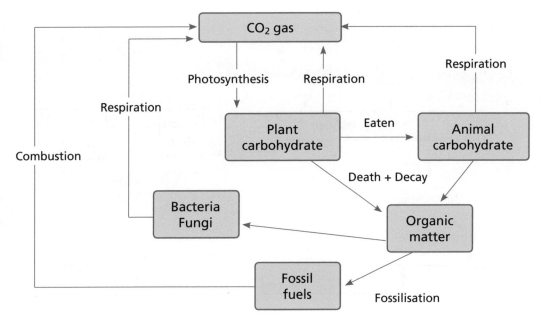

Figure 1.8 Carbon cycle

The nitrogen cycle

Introduction
The nitrogen cycle describes the changes in the forms of nitrogen that occur in nature. The cycle is essential for the survival of organisms.

- Nitrogen is a vital component of amino acids and proteins.
- Proteins (in the form of enzymes) control metabolism in all living things.
- Almost 80 per cent of the atmosphere is made up of nitrogen gas (N_2). In this form it cannot be used by plants or animals.
- Bacteria in the nitrogen cycle convert nitrogen gas in the air to nitrate (NO_3^-). This process is called nitrogen fixation. Nitrates can then be absorbed by the roots of plants and used to make protein.
- Animals consume the plants, converting the nutrients to animal protein.
- Nitrification is the addition of oxygen to nitrogen compounds.
- Denitrification is the removal of oxygen from nitrogen compounds.
- Bacteria play a large role in the nitrogen cycle (see fig. 1.9).

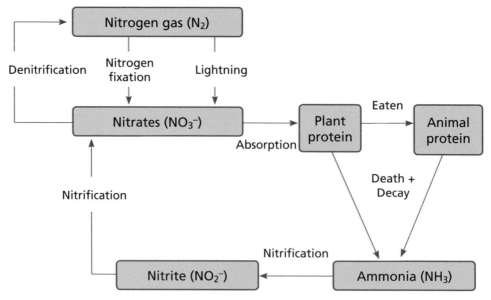

Figure 1.9 Nitrogen cycle

Nitrogen fixation

Nitrogen fixation is the term given to the conversion of nitrogen to nitrates. It is brought about by two processes.

- Lightning
- Bacteria

One type of bacterium that carries out nitrogen fixation is found on the nodules of the roots of legumes (clover, pea and bean plants). It fixes nitrogen for the plant, while in return the plant supplies sugars to the bacterium. Such a relationship in nature where two different organisms live together is called **symbiosis**. When the association is beneficial to both, the relationship is known as **mutualism**.

Human population

Since 1700 there has been a huge increase in human population. The main reasons for this huge increase are:

- the large reduction in child mortality
- an improvement in life expectancy.

Because of these factors, more of the population reach the reproductive age and produce offspring.

The improved life expectancy is due to:

1. **Reduction of disease**

   Several important scientific advances have reduced disease.

   - Immunisation, vaccination and antibiotics considerably improved the health of the population.
   - The improvement in sanitation and public health.
   - Water treatment and proper sewage disposal removed many sources of disease.

2. **Increase in food supply**

   Good agricultural practices improved the quality and quantity of produce.

   - High-yielding strains or breeds of plants and animals were developed.
   - The development and use of artificial fertilisers and herbicides further improved yields.

Control of human population

The world's population growth must begin to decline. Resources are limited. A lower level of population would ultimately allow for a better quality of life with sufficient resources for all.

It is thought that education and birth control in developed countries have largely stabilised populations. In developing countries problems with population include:

- many people still wish to have traditionally large families
- shortages of doctors and trained medical staff to explain family planning techniques
- some cultures are suspicious of contraception.

key point

Four main factors that reduce human population:

- Famine
- War
- Disease
- Contraception

Human impact on an ecosystem

Pollution

A **pollutant** may be physical (noise, heat, radiation) or chemical (industrial or biological wastes) that can cause harm to organisms in the environment.

Pollution is the release of substances or energy into the environment in large quantities that harm the natural inhabitants.

Air pollution

One form of air pollution is caused by the industrial release of **greenhouse gases** into the atmosphere. Greenhouse gases reduce the ability of the earth to reflect heat radiation back into space. The greenhouse effect is causing a steady increase in the temperature of the earth and the atmosphere.

Causes

The most important greenhouse gases are carbon dioxide, methane and chlorofluorocarbons (CFCs).

- Carbon dioxide gas is released when fossil fuels are burned. Since the Industrial Revolution, the increasing use of fossil fuels for energy has produced a steady rise in the levels of carbon dioxide in the atmosphere. Many scientists link this increase to climate change.
- Methane is even more efficient than carbon dioxide at retaining heat in the atmosphere. Methane is released in large quantities from cattle and pigs. Landfill dumping is also a source of methane.
- CFCs were used as a liquid coolant in refrigerators. CFCs destroy the protective ozone layer in the upper atmosphere.

Effects

The effects of global warming are thought to cause:

- The rise of sea levels
- The melting of polar ice
- A change in weather patterns.

Control

Efforts to reduce global warming include the following:

- Many countries have signed up to international agreements to limit the use of fossil fuels.
- New sources of renewable energy are being developed and refined. Wind and solar energy are two examples.
- New engines for transport are being developed. Hydrogen can be used to fuel car engines, with water being the only waste product.
- Policies to increase public awareness of the importance and the means of energy conservation are being developed.

Conservation

Conservation is a series of measures designed to retain viable populations of species in their ecosystems.

Human activities such as agriculture, urbanisation and industrialisation can contribute to ecosystem damage.

Conservation in the fishing industry

The scale of fishing around Britain and Ireland has seriously depleted stocks of many species. A ban on fishing for certain species has had some success in increasing population numbers. Legislation by the European Union to conserve stocks include:

- limiting the size of fishing fleets
- reducing the number of days at sea by trawlers
- increasing the mesh size of nets.

Waste management

Urban communities produce huge quantities of household and commercial waste. The traditional method of waste disposal was by dumping the rubbish in landfill sites, such as disused quarries and gravel pits. This method leads to three main problems.

- There are insufficient sites to accommodate all the rubbish.
- When compacted and removed from air, carbon-based waste releases large amounts of the greenhouse gas methane.
- Toxic substances can leach into groundwater, presenting a threat to human supplies.

Waste minimisation

Many projects to minimise waste have been introduced.
Waste minimisation can be done by the following:

- Separating household rubbish so that many materials can be recycled. Cardboard, paper, some plastic, aluminium cans and glass can be recycled.
- Organic waste can be composted to produce natural organic fertiliser.
- Most old electrical items such as TVs, fridges, cookers, etc. can all be stripped to recycle parts.
- The remaining rubbish that cannot be recycled can be incinerated to reduce volume.

Waste from farming

The overuse of **chemical fertilisers** on land can result in algal bloom pollution of waterways. Nutrient Management Planning can minimise risks by specifying correct usage of fertilisers in particular areas.

Waste from forestry

The planting of conifers close to streams and rivers can cause pollution. Falling needles (leaves) decrease the pH of water, causing harm to aquatic plants and animals. Planting of trees away from waterways can reduce potential pollution.

Sewage

Sewage treatment is a process that uses micro-organisms to remove its harmful components. The main stages of sewage treatment are summarised in fig. 1.10.

Sewage is a liquid waste produced in large quantities in urban areas. The discharge of raw sewage into the environment could cause serious pollution problems.

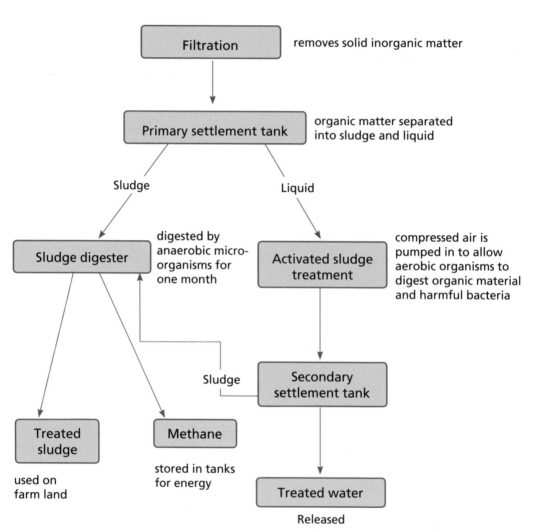

Figure 1.10 Stages in sewage treatment

1.5 Study of an Ecosystem Guidelines

The following points are to be used merely as a checklist for the procedures and exercises that are required to be carried out in the Study of an Ecosystem. Each student, under the supervision of their teacher, should:

- Select and visit one ecosystem.
- Provide a broad overview of the ecosystem chosen.
- Identify five plants and five animals in the ecosystem (Qualitative Survey).
- Locate and identify the different habitats present.
- Describe the use of various apparatus used to collect plants and animals.
- Conduct a quantitative study of plants using frequency and percentage cover techniques in a selected area of the ecosystem.
- Conduct a quantitative study of animals in a selected area.
- Present results in the forms of graphs, tables, diagrams, etc.
- Identify possible sources of error in the surveys carried out.
- Investigate three abiotic factors in the habitat and relate the findings to the distribution of organisms.
- Identify an adaptation of any organism to conditions in the habitat.
- Construct a food chain, food web and a pyramid of numbers in the habitat.
- Prepare a report of conclusions drawn from the results of the study.

2016 Q1 HIGHER LEVEL

1. Explain **five** of the following terms.

    (a) Ecology.   (d) Contest competition.
    (b) Symbiosis.   (e) Edaphic.
    (c) Nutrient recycling.   (f) Biotic.

LEAVING CERT MARKING SCHEME

1. 2(7) + 3(2) i.e. best five answers from (a) – (f)

    (a) *Ecology:* The study of (the various interactions between) organisms and their environment
    (b) *Symbiosis:* (A relationship) between species in which at least one benefits

(c) *Nutrient* recycling: Reuse (of nutrients)

(d) *Contest competition:* A struggle for a resource in which only one wins

(e) *Edaphic:* (Relating to) soil

(f) *Biotic:* (Relating to) living (organisms)

2016 Q10 (c) HIGHER LEVEL

10. (c) A typical grazing food chain, consisting of four trophic levels, is shown below. Each letter represents a different species.

A → B → C → D

(i)   What is meant by the term 'trophic level'?

(ii) Explain why food chains are generally short.

(iii) Which letter represents the secondary consumer?

(iv) Give a possible reason why the population of C may decline naturally.

(v)   Suggest a possible consequence for the population of A if the population of C was significantly reduced. Explain your answer.

(vi) Suggest how members of species D might respond, if the population of C was significantly reduced.

(vii) A food web is a series of interconnected food chains. Suggest how it may be possible for the secondary consumer, in the food chain above, to be a primary consumer in another food chain.   **(24)**

LEAVING CERT MARKING SCHEME

10. (c) (i) *Trophic level:* Position on the food chain **or** feeding level **or** energy level **or** feeding stage   **(3)**

(ii) *Why chains short:* Little (10%) energy passed on to next level **or** large amount (90%) of energy lost at each level   **(3)**

(iii) *Secondary consumer:* *C   **(3)**

(iv) *Why C might decline:* Predation **or** increase in D **or** disease **or** lack of food **or** lack of B **or** migration   **(3)**

(v)   *Consequence:* (Population A) falls   **(3)**

Explanation: Population of primary consumers increases **or** population of B increases (which eat large amount of produce A)   **(3)**

(vi) *How D might respond:* Migrate **or** switch prey.   **(3)**

(vii) *How possible primary consumer in other food chain:* It may be an omnivore **or** explained   **(3)**

UNIT 2

The Cell

2.1 Cell Structure

Microscopy

The **light microscope** is used to observe and magnify prepared slides. The slide is placed on the stage and the fine and coarse adjusters are used to focus the image produced in the eyepiece. The light microscope can be used to view living specimens although its magnification is limited.

The **Transmission Electron Microscope** (TEM) is capable of much higher magnifications, even to view the structure of DNA molecules. The TEM is not capable of providing images of living organisms.

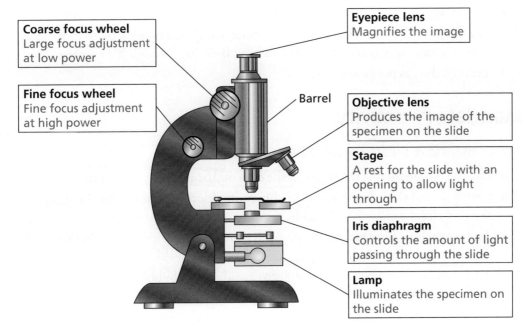

Coarse focus wheel
Large focus adjustment at low power

Fine focus wheel
Fine focus adjustment at high power

Barrel

Eyepiece lens
Magnifies the image

Objective lens
Produces the image of the specimen on the slide

Stage
A rest for the slide with an opening to allow light through

Iris diaphragm
Controls the amount of light passing through the slide

Lamp
Illuminates the specimen on the slide

Figure 2.1 The light microscope

Magnification

The magnification of an object is the product of the magnification of the eyepiece and the objective lens.

Eyepiece Lens	Objective Lens	Magnification
×10	×10	10 × 10 = 100
×10	×40	10 × 40 = 400

Mandatory activity

To make slides of animal and plant cells and observe under a microscope

Preparation of the slide

- A very thin slice (thin enough for light to pass through) of the specimen is placed on a clean glass slide with a drop of water.
- A cover slip is placed over the specimen (carefully, to prevent the entry of any air bubbles).
- Staining is done to highlight different structures in the specimen.
  - Iodine is added to onion cells to highlight the nucleus and starch grains.
  - Methylene blue is used to highlight the nucleus and cytoplasm of cheek cells.

Precautions using the microscope

- Never touch electric light sources, as they can cause burns.
- When focusing at low power (× 100), use the coarse adjuster before finishing focusing with the fine adjuster.

- At high power (× 400), always bring the lens and stage to near contact while viewing from the side. Focusing is then done using the fine adjuster to move the slide and lens away from one another while observing through the eyepiece.
- Treat all dyes as poisonous.

Mandatory activity

To prepare a slide of an animal cell

- Use the blunt end of a match to scrape cells off the inside of the **cheek**.
- Gently spread the cells (to avoid crushing) on a clean glass slide and allow drying in the air to fix the cells onto the slide.
- Add **methylene blue** for one minute and gently rinse off using dripping water. This stains the nucleus and the cytoplasm.
- Add a cover slip carefully, at an angle, to avoid any air bubbles.

Mandatory activity

To prepare a slide of a plant cell

- Peel a single layer of cells from an **onion**.
- Place the sample onto a slide with a drop of water, carefully, to avoid air bubbles.
- Add some **iodine** to stain the nucleus and the vacuole.
- Add a cover slip carefully, at an angle, to avoid any air bubbles.

Drawings of each type of cell as seen under the light microscope are shown in fig. 2.2.

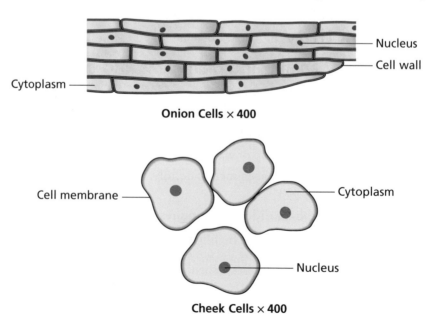

Figure 2.2 Plant and animal cells using the light microscope

Cell ultrastructure

With the higher magnification possible using an electron microscope, many different cell **organelles** can be identified (fig. 2.3).

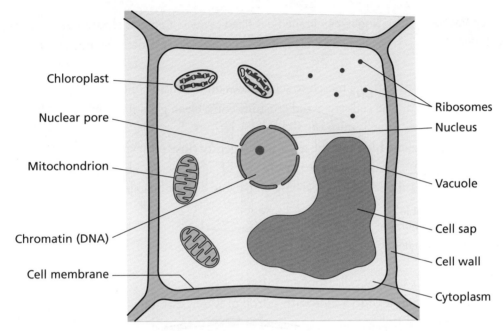

Chloroplast

Nuclear pore

Mitochondrion

Chromatin (DNA)

Cell membrane

Ribosomes

Nucleus

Vacuole

Cell sap

Cell wall

Cytoplasm

Figure 2.3 Plant cell

Organelle	Structure	Function
Nucleus	Surrounded by a double membrane with many pores. Contains chromosomes (DNA) in the form of chromatin	Stores genetic information (DNA) and controls all activities in the cell
Ribosome	Made of protein and RNA	Protein synthesis
Mitochondrion	Double membrane with inner foldings of cristae (see fig. 2.4)	Krebs cycle and hydrogen carrier systems of aerobic respiration occur here
Cell Membrane	A phospholipid bilayer with protein (see fig. 2.6)	Acts as a selectively permeable barrier
Cytosol	Liquid portion of the cytoplasm outside the nucleus	Provides a liquid medium for enzymes
Cytoplasm	Matrix surrounding the nucleus in which organelles are suspended	Support for organelles

Organelle	Structure	Function
Organelles Only Present in Plant Cells		
Chloroplast	Double membrane with inner folds of lamellae and grana containing chlorophyll (see fig. 2.5)	Carries out photosynthesis
Large Vacuole	Single-membrane fluid-filled cavity	Contains food stored as cell sap
Cell Wall	Fully permeable wall of cellulose	Provides strength and support

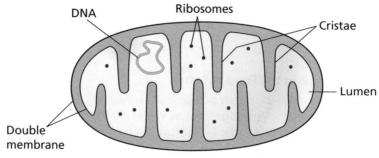

Figure 2.4 Mitochondrion

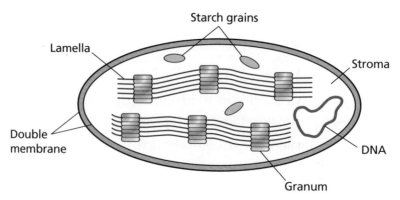

Figure 2.5 Chloroplast

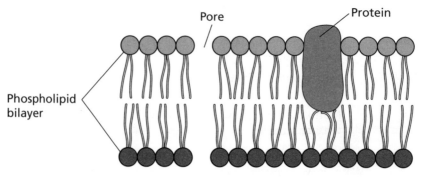

Figure 2.6 Cell membrane

Movement through cell membranes

The cell membrane is a **selectively permeable barrier**. A number of different mechanisms are used to transport materials across membranes.

Osmosis and diffusion

Osmosis is the movement of water from a high concentration to a low concentration across a selectively permeable membrane. No energy is required for osmosis.

Plant root hairs absorb water from the soil by osmosis.

Application of Osmosis in the Food Industry
The high sugar concentration in jam acts as a preservative, as it prevents the growth of micro-organisms. The sugar draws water from the cells of the micro-organisms by osmosis. This prevents their growth and reproduction.

Diffusion is the movement of a substance from its region of high concentration to its region of low concentration along a diffusion gradient. Diffusion does not require energy.

Oxygen gas in the lungs moves across the alveoli into the blood capillaries by diffusion.

Turgor and plasmolysis

Many plants use lignified xylem cells (wood) to support their aerial parts.

- Non-woody green plants do not have this support.
- Non-woody plants pack their cells and vacuoles with water by osmosis.
- Cells in this condition are said to be fully **turgid**.

If a green plant is not watered for a number of days, the cells lose their water and the plants wilt due to the loss of turgidity and support (see fig. 2.7).

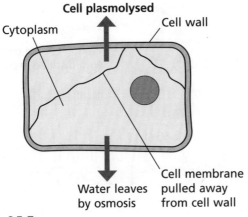
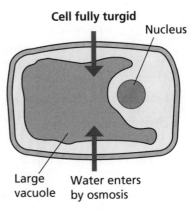

Cell plasmolysed
Cytoplasm
Cell wall
Water leaves by osmosis
Cell membrane pulled away from cell wall

Cell fully turgid
Nucleus
Large vacuole
Water enters by osmosis

Figure 2.7 Turgor

Mandatory activity

Conduct any activity to demonstrate osmosis

1. Soak two 50 cm strips of Visking (dialysis) tubing in water for ten minutes to soften them.
2. Tie a knot at one end of each strip.
3. Half fill one strip with an 80 per cent sucrose solution and the other with distilled water.
4. Tie a second knot at the open end of each strip and rinse each under the tap.
5. **Dry** each strip with paper towels.
6. Place each strip on a balance and record their mass.
7. Observe each strip and record their turgidity.
8. Place each strip in separate labelled **beakers of distilled water and leave for 15 minutes** (see fig. 2.8).
9. Remove the strips and dry as before.
10. Record the mass of each and their turgidity.
11. Repeat points 8 to 10 twice more.

Expected results

The mass and turgidity of the Visking tubing with sucrose solution should increase with time. The Visking tubing with distilled water (the control) should show no change.

Important points to remember

- The Visking tubing acts as a semi-permeable barrier. The smaller water molecules can pass through, but sugar molecules cannot.
- The distilled water in the beaker is the high concentration of water. The sucrose solution in the Visking tubing is the low concentration of water. This difference is what causes osmosis to occur.

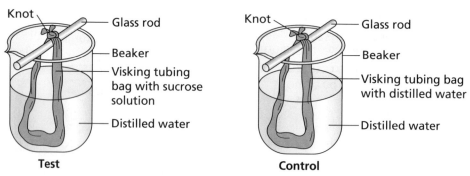

Figure 2.8 Osmosis in an artificial cell

Eukaryotic and prokaryotic cells

Animal, plant and fungi cells all have their nuclear material (DNA) stored in a nuclear membrane sac. Such cells are known as **eukaryotic**.

Bacteria are described as **prokaryotic** organisms. They are much smaller than eukaryots and their nuclear material is not bound by a membrane but spread around the cytoplasm.

Differences between Eukaryotic and Prokaryotic Organisms

Eukaryotic	Prokaryotic
1. Membrane-bound nucleus separating it from cytoplasm	1. Nuclear material spread around organism in ring shapes
2. Larger cell with many membrane-bound organelles	2. Smaller with no membrane-bound organelles
3. Cell wall, if present, made of cellulose or chitin	3. Cell wall made of protein

2011 Q14 (c) HIGHER LEVEL

14. (c) (i) State the precise location of the cell membrane in plant cells.
   (ii) With what type of cell do you associate membrane-bound organelles?
   (iii) What corresponding term is used to describe bacterial cells?
   (iv) The cell membrane is described as being *selectively permeable*. What does this mean?
   (v) Why is diffusion alternatively known as *passive transport*?
   (vi) Osmosis may be described as 'a special case of diffusion'. Explain why.
   (vii) Describe, with the aid of a labelled diagram, how you demonstrated osmosis in the laboratory.
   (viii) Name the structure by which *Amoeba* gets rid of excess water that has entered by osmosis.

LEAVING CERT MARKING SCHEME

14. (c) (i) Immediately inside the cell wall   (3)
   (ii) *Eukaryotic   (3)
   (iii) *Prokaryotic   (3)
   (iv) Only some substances are allowed through   (3)

(v) No (or little) energy (or ATP) required (3)

(vi) Movement of water **or** (osmosis) requires a membrane (3)

(vii) *Diagram:* Container + 2 solutions separated by a membrane (3,0)

Labels: Membrane **or** plant tissue / solution 1 indicated / solution 2 indicated (3[1])

Result: Shown in diagram or stated (3)

(viii) Contractile vacuole (3)

Enzymes

Definitions

- Metabolism
- Enzyme
- Substrate
- Active site
- Enzyme saturation
- Substrate
- Denaturation
- Immobilised enzymes
- Bioprocessing
- Bioprocessors (bioreactors)

Outline

- Structure and nature of enzymes
- Role of enzymes in organisms
- Effect of temperature and pH ranges on enzyme activity (with graphs)
- Applications of immobilised enzymes
- Induced fit theory of enzyme action
- Optimum activity of enzymes under specific conditions of pH and temperature
- Heat denaturation of proteins (enzymes)

Practical Activities

- Investigate the effect of pH on enzyme activity
- Investigate the effect of temperature on enzyme activity
- Investigate the effect of heat denaturation on enzyme activity (HL)
- Prepare one enzyme immobilisation and examine its application

Each type of enzyme is made up of a long chain of amino acids with a secondary structure that provides it with a unique folded shape. This shape provides the enzyme with a specific **active site**.

IMPORTANT DEFINITIONS

Enzymes: Biological catalysts, protein in nature, and control metabolic reactions.

Active site: The point on an enzyme of temporary attachment to the substrate. It is specific.

Denatured enzyme: Loss of activity due to an irreversible change in enzyme structure (active site). It is caused by heat, pH change, etc.

Enzyme saturation: Enzyme functioning at a maximum rate under specific circumstances. The rate cannot increase, even if more substrate is added, unless enzyme concentration is increased.

Substrate: A substance that attaches to the enzyme at the active site. It is converted to product(s) and released.

Factors affecting enzyme activity

pH

- Most enzymes function in a near neutral pH $= 7$ (see fig. 2.9).
- Outside this range, most enzymes tend to denature, i.e. the active site changes shape and it can no longer function.
- An exception is the enzyme pepsin, found in the stomach. It can function at a **pH of 1.5**.

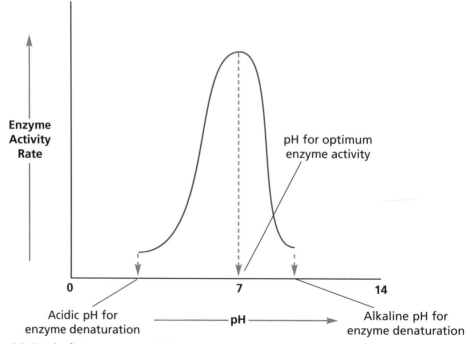

Figure 2.9 Graph of pH vs enzyme activity rate

Temperature

Enzymes can only function in a fluid environment.

- In solid ice an enzyme has an activity rate of zero.
- The rate of enzyme action increases as the temperature increases up to a limit of around 40 °C (for warm-blooded animals). Above that temperature the enzyme becomes denatured.
- Plant enzymes often have an optimum temperature of around 25 °C (see fig. 2.10).

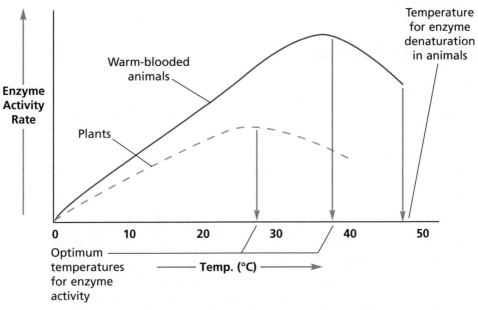

Figure 2.10 Graph of temp (°C) vs enzyme activity rate

Enzyme action (How an enzyme works)

The **induced fit theory** of enzyme action describes how the enzyme slightly changes shape so that its active site perfectly fits the substrate.

- The enzyme and substrate temporarily bind together, forming the enzyme–substrate complex.
- The binding action converts the substrate to products, which are then released.
- The enzyme is now free to repeat the process (see fig. 2.11).

> **key point**
>
> The active site of any one enzyme can only facilitate one type of substrate. This is why enzymes are said to be specific.

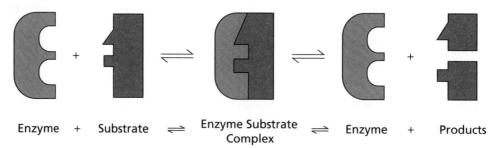

Enzyme + Substrate ⇌ Enzyme Substrate Complex ⇌ Enzyme + Products

Figure 2.11 Enzyme action

Mandatory activity

To investigate the effect of pH on the rate of enzyme activity

1. Chop a **celery stalk** (*source of enzyme catalax*) into pieces of equal size.
2. Using a balance, weigh out 5 g of celery.
3. Add the celery to a graduated cylinder.
4. Add 20 cm^3 of **buffer solution** (pH = 7) to the same graduated cylinder.
5. Add one drop of washing-up liquid to the graduated cylinder using a dropper.
6. Using a micro pipette, add 2 cm^3 of **hydrogen peroxide** to a test tube.
7. Place the graduated cylinder and the test tube in a water bath at 25 °C (see fig. 2.12).
8. Leave for ten minutes to adjust to the new temperature.
9. Carefully pour the hydrogen peroxide into the graduated cylinder.
10. Note and record the volume in the cylinder immediately.
11. Read the volume again after five minutes and record.
12. Subtract the initial volume from the final volume to calculate the **volume of foam** formed. Record the result.
13. Repeat the above procedures for buffer solutions of pH 4 and 10.
14. A graph should be drawn of enzyme activity (volume of foam after two minutes) against pH. Place pH on the horizontal axis.

Expected results

The greatest enzyme activity (volume of foam per unit time) would be expected around pH = 7. Enzyme activity would decrease in buffer solutions at the extremes of the pH scale, due to enzyme denaturation.

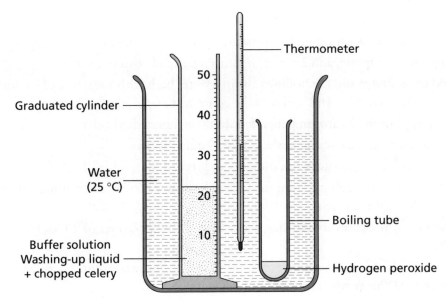

Figure 2.12 Setting up the experiment

Important points to remember

- **Enzyme** = catalase (from celery), **substrate** = hydrogen peroxide, **products** = water and oxygen gas.
- **Independent or manipulated variable** = pH, by using different buffer solutions.
- **Dependent variable** = rate of enzyme activity, measured by recording volume of foam produced per unit time (ml/min).
- **Controlled variables:**
  - (i) **Enzyme concentration:** Using equal weights of similarly sized chopped celery.
  - (ii) **Substrate concentration:** Using equal volumes of the same hydrogen peroxide solution.
  - (iii) **Temperature:** Using a water bath and thermometer.

Control experiment: Same as above with celery that has been boiled in water for 15 minutes. (This denatures the enzyme, catalase.)

Mandatory activity

To investigate the effect of temperature on the rate of enzyme activity

1. Chop a celery stalk into pieces of equal size.
2. Using a balance, weigh out 5 g of the celery.
3. Add the celery to a graduated cylinder.

4. Add 20 cm^3 of buffer solution to the same graduated cylinder.

5. Add one drop of washing-up liquid to the graduated cylinder using a dropper.

6. Using a micro pipette, add 2 cm^3 of hydrogen peroxide to a test tube.

7. Stand the cylinder and the boiling tube in a water bath with a mixture of ice and water for ten minutes. This will cool the contents to 0 °C (see fig. 2.13).

8. Carefully pour the hydrogen peroxide into the graduated cylinder.

9. Note and record the volume in the cylinder immediately.

10. Read the volume again after five minutes and record.

11. Subtract the initial volume from the final volume to calculate the volume of foam formed. Record the result.

12. Repeat the procedures above using water baths at temperatures of 20 °C, 40 °C and 60 °C.

13. Draw a graph of enzyme activity (volume of foam after two minutes) against temperature. Put temperature on the horizontal axis.

Expected results

The greatest enzyme activity (volume of foam per unit time) would be expected around a temperature of 25–30 °C. Enzyme activity would decrease at higher temperatures due to heat denaturation. At 0 °C (ice) enzyme activity ceases.

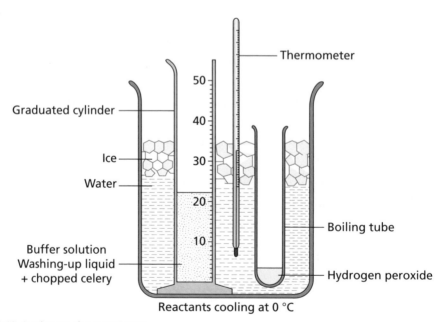

Figure 2.13 Setting up the experiment

Important points to remember

- **Enzyme** = catalase (from celery), **substrate** = hydrogen peroxide, **products** = water and oxygen gas.
- **Independent or manipulated variable** = temperature, using water bath and thermometer.
- **Dependent variable** = rate of enzyme activity, measured by recording volume of foam produced per unit time (ml/min).
- **Controlled variables:**
  - (i) **Enzyme concentration:** Using equal weights of similarly sized chopped celery.
  - (ii) **Substrate concentration:** Using equal volumes of the same hydrogen peroxide solution.
  - (iii) **pH:** Using the same buffer solution.

Control experiment: Same as above with celery that has been boiled in water for 15 minutes. (This denatures the enzyme, catalase.)

Mandatory activity

To investigate the effect of heat denaturation on catalase activity

1. Place 5 g of chopped celery into a boiling tube.
2. Place the boiling tube in a boiling water bath for ten minutes.
3. Remove the boiling tube and allow it to cool.
4. Add 20 cm^3 of buffer solution to a graduated cylinder.
5. Using a dropper, add one drop of washing-up liquid.
6. Add the denatured celery to the graduated cylinder.
7. Add 2 cm^3 of hydrogen peroxide to a test tube.
8. Place the test tube and the graduated cylinder in a water bath at 25 °C (see fig. 2.14).
9. Record the presence or absence of foam.
10. Repeat the procedure from step 4 using 5 g of 'live' unheated celery.

Expected results

The 'boiled celery' should show no activity, due to the heat denaturation of catalase. The 'live' unheated celery should produce bubbles of oxygen.

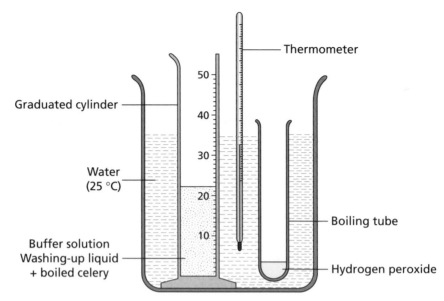

Figure 2.14 Setting up the experiment

Enzyme immobilisation

This describes a procedure to extract useful enzymes, usually from micro-organisms.

- After removal, the enzymes are then stabilised so that they can be repeatedly used to catalyse chemical reactions.
- The enzymes can then produce large quantities of useful products.

Biotechnology

Techniques using micro-organisms, or their enzymes, to produce useful products in medicine or industry.

Advantages of enzyme immobilisation

- Easy recovery of enzymes for reuse.
- Easy harvesting of products (no enzyme contamination).
- Greater enzyme stability.

DEFINITIONS

- **Continuous flow bioprocessing** involves the regular addition of nutrients to immobilised enzymes or micro-organisms in a bioprocessor (bioreactor). This produces a continuous flow of product.
- **Batch processing** is the addition of a fixed amount of nutrients to micro-organisms at the beginning of a process. On completion the product and micro-organisms are separated from the mix.

Applications of enzyme immobilisation

- **The production of fructose for use in canned drinks**. Fructose is sweeter than glucose or sucrose, so it is preferred for sweetened drinks. The enzyme glucose isomerase converts glucose to fructose. This enzyme is difficult to produce, so it is reused through enzyme immobilisation.
- **To make lactose-free milk**. Many people are lactose intolerant. They cannot produce the enzyme lactase that breaks lactose down. Immobilised lactase is used to remove lactose from milk.
- **Clarification of fruit juices**. Fruit juices contain binding carbohydrates called pectins. These can make the juices more viscous and cause cloudiness. Immobilised pectinase is used to remove pectins from fruit juices.
- **Production of vinegar**. Bacteria are immobilised to convert ethyl alcohol and oxygen to acetic acid or vinegar.
- **Diagnostic reagents**. Dipsticks with the immobilised enzyme glucose oxidase can be used to test for glucose concentrations in blood samples.

Mandatory activity

To prepare an enzyme immobilisation and examine its application

1. Add 0.4 g of **sodium alginate** to 10 cm^3 of water.
2. Mix 2 g of yeast in 10 cm^3 of distilled water and leave for five minutes.
3. Prepare 1.4 per cent **calcium chloride** solution and place in a tall beaker.
4. Mix the alginate solution and the yeast suspension and draw the mixture into a **syringe**.
5. From a height of about 10 cm, release the mixture from the syringe, one drop at a time, into the calcium chloride. Each drop will form a bead (see fig. 2.15).
6. Leave the beads to harden for 20 minutes.
7. **Filter the beads**, wash with distilled water and place into a separating funnel (A) (see fig. 2.16).
8. Mix another 2 g of yeast with 10 cm^3 of distilled water.
9. Pour this mixture into a second separating funnel (B).
10. Make a 100 ml solution of 1 per cent sucrose and heat to 40 °C.
11. Pour 50 cm^3 of this solution into each of the separating funnels.
12. Immediately **dip Clinstix strips** into samples taken from each separating funnel.
13. Remove the strips, leave for ten seconds, and compare both strips with the colour card supplied.
14. Repeat the test every 30 seconds.

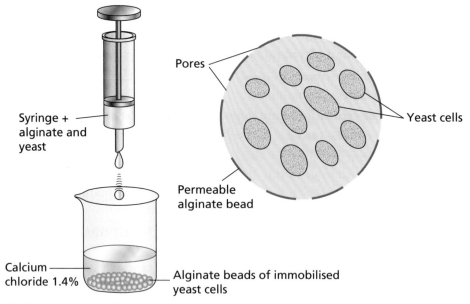

Figure 2.15 Enzyme immobilisation

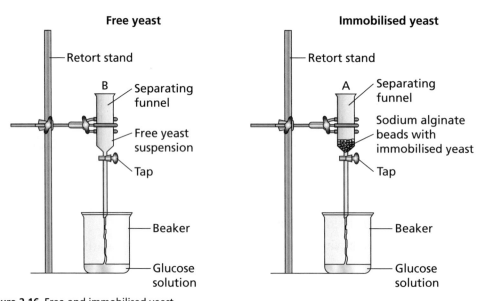

Figure 2.16 Free and immobilised yeast

Expected results

- The samples released from the separating funnel with the 'free' yeast (B) are more turbid (cloudy) due to the presence of the yeast cells.
- The 'free' yeast cells break down the sucrose at a faster rate than the immobilised cells.

Important points to remember

- **Enzyme** = enzymes in yeast cells, **substrate** = sucrose, **products** = glucose.
- **Independent or manipulated variable** = yeast cells in beads and free yeast cells.
- **Dependent variable** = rate of glucose formation.
- **Controlled variables:**
  - (i) **Enzyme concentration:** Equal amounts (2 g) of yeast cells.
  - (ii) **Substrate concentration:** Equal volumes of the same sucrose solution.
  - (iii) **Temperature:** Sucrose solutions at 40 °C.

Note

- The darker pink or more purple the strip, the greater the quantity of glucose present.
- The use of Clinstix is **a quantitative** test for glucose. The colour changes indicate the quantity of glucose present.
- The enzymes in the yeast cells break down the disaccharide sucrose to its monosaccharides.

2015 Q7 (c) HIGHER LEVEL

HL

7. (c)(i) In relation to an investigation you carried out into heat denaturation of an enzyme, answer the following:
   1. Name the enzyme you used.
   2. Name the enzyme's substrate.
   3. Name the product(s) formed.

   (ii) How did you denature the enzyme?
   (iii) How did you know that the enzyme had been denatured?
   (iv) Why are buffers needed when carrying out experiments with enzymes in school?

LEAVING CERT MARKING SCHEME

7. (c) 8 + 8 + 2(1)

7. (c)(i)

1. Catalase		Pepsin (or protease)		Amylase (or diastase)
2. Hydrogen peroxide	**or** Protein		**or**	Starch
3. Oxygen (and water)		Peptides (or amino acids)		Maltose

   (ii) Boil **or** heat to high temperature (≥ 60°C)
   (iii) Negative result for named test for product **or** positive result for named test for substrate [*must match enzyme or produce in c(i) above*]
   (iv) To maintain (a constant) pH **or** to vary pH

Photosynthesis

Definitions

- Photosynthesis
- Anabolic reaction
- Phosphorylation
- Photophosphorylation
- Reduction (of NADP)

Outline

- Photosynthesis and its role in nature
- Balanced equation of photosynthesis
- Sources of light, carbon dioxide and water in the leaf
- Adaptations of the leaf for photosynthesis
- Formation of oxygen gas
- Formation of carbohydrate
- Location of chlorophyll in cells
- Use of artificial light, controlled carbon dioxide and temperature levels, in greenhouse cultivation
- The roles of chlorophyll, carbon dioxide and the splitting of water in photosynthesis

- Detailed structure and functions of the energy molecules
  - NADH and NADPH
  - ADP/ATP
- Light stage I (cyclic) and light stage II (non-cyclic) of the light dependent stages
- Photolysis of water/NADPH and ATP formation
- Dark stage and the roles of ATP and NADPH

Practical Activity

- Investigate the influence of light intensity or carbon dioxide concentration on the rate of photosynthesis

Role of photosynthesis in nature

- Photosynthesis provides food (energy) for plants.
- All animals depend directly or indirectly on plant photosynthesis for their food (energy).
- Photosynthesis removes carbon dioxide from the air and produces oxygen gas for aerobic respiration in both plants and animals.

key point

Photosynthesis is an example of an anabolic chemical reaction. Such a reaction requires energy to make complex biomolecules from simple inorganic molecules.

Photosynthesis can be summarised by the balanced chemical equation:

$$6CO_2 + 6H_2O + \text{sunlight energy} \xrightarrow{\text{chlorophyll}} C_6H_{12}O_6 + 6O_2$$

Word equation for photosynthesis

$$\text{carbon dioxide} + \text{water} \xrightarrow[\text{chlorophyll}]{\text{sunlight}} \text{glucose} + \text{oxygen}$$

Adaptations of the leaf for photosynthesis

- Large surface area to capture light energy
- Very thin to facilitate gaseous exchange
- **Stomata** on the lower epidermis to control gaseous exchange
- Large numbers of **chloroplasts** in the palisade layer at the upper surface to capture light
- Leaf veins of xylem and phloem for transport

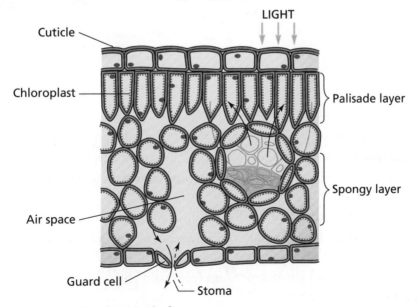

Figure 2.17 Transverse section through a leaf

Energy in the cell

Organisms must store energy so that it is available when required. The only means of storing energy in the cells is in chemical form, that is, in chemical bonds.

ATP

Adenosine triphosphate (ATP) is a molecule that stores energy in cells.

When a cell requires energy, ATP is converted to ADP + P, releasing energy. Energy from respiration is stored when ADP + P join to form ATP. This process is called **phosphorylation** (see fig. 2.18).

 ### ATP

Adenosine triphosphate is made up of adenine (amino acid), ribose (sugar) and three phosphate molecules. The energy is stored in the electrons of the chemical bonds linking the phosphate molecules.

NADH

NADH (Nicotinamide Adenine Dinucleotide) and **NADPH** (Nicotinamide Adenine Dinucleotide Phosphate) are two molecules also involved in the storage of energy in the cell. They store and transfer hydrogen ions, energy and electrons for metabolism.

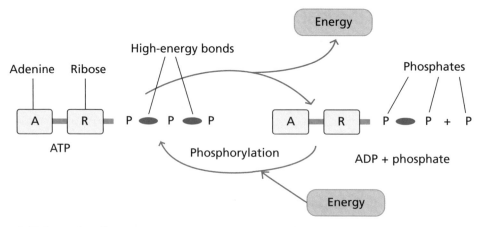

Figure 2.18 Energy in cells

Biochemistry of photosynthesis

The process of photosynthesis results in the splitting of water, releasing:

- Oxygen (used for respiration or released to the atmosphere)
- Hydrogen and electrons (which are combined with carbon dioxide gas to form carbohydrate)

 The process of photosynthesis can be divided into two stages.

- **Light stage**, which is dependent on the presence of light and occurs in the **grana** of the chloroplast.
- **Dark stage**, which is light-independent (goes on night and day) and occurs in the **stroma** of the chloroplast.

1. Light stage

This occurs in two parts:

(a) Light stage I (cyclic)

(b) Light stage II (non-cyclic).

Light stage I

- Light energy trapped by **chlorophyll** is passed to an electron.
- The electron moves to an electron acceptor and is passed through a number of carriers.
- Energy is released at each step and used to form ATP.
- The electron finally returns to the chlorophyll. See fig. 2.19.

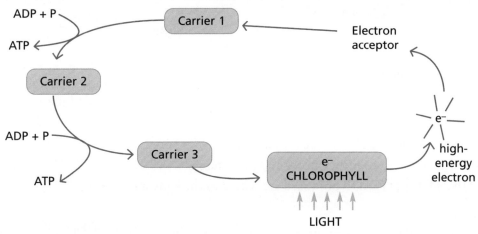

Figure 2.19 Light stage I

Light stage II

- Light energy trapped by chlorophyll is passed to **two electrons**.
- The two electrons leave the chlorophyll and move to an electron acceptor.
- Both electrons join with **NADP** (nicotinamide adenine dinucleotide phosphate).
- The NADP^{--} then causes H_2O to split (photolysis), releasing oxygen, two electrons and two H$^+$ ions.
  - The oxygen can be used for respiration or released as waste.
  - The electrons are passed through carriers, releasing energy to form **ATP**.
  - The hydrogen atoms released when water is split reduce NADP to NADPH. See fig. 2.20.

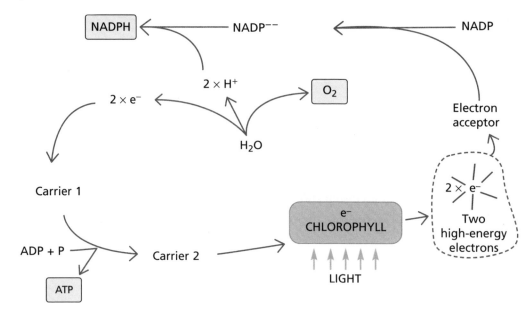

Figure 2.20 Light stage II

2. Dark stage
- **ATP and NADPH** produced in the light stage are used.
- CO_2 is reduced to form glucose and then starch.
- The ADP and NADP produced are reused in the light stage (see fig. 2.21).

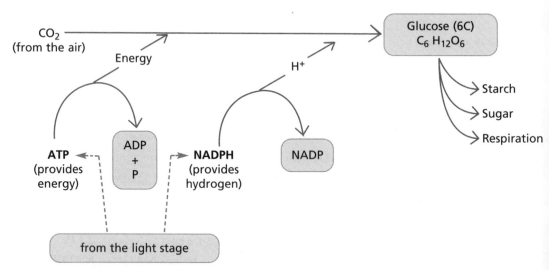

Figure 2.21 Dark stage

Mandatory activity

To investigate the effect of light intensity on the rate of photosynthesis

1. Cut a fresh stem of **Elodea** at an **angle** with a **wet blade** (this facilitates the release of bubbles) and place in a test tube with a solution of excess sodium bicarbonate.
2. Place the test tube in a beaker of water with a thermometer. This is to check that the temperature does not vary.
3. Set a lamp beside the beaker. Set the distance from the lamp to the test tube with the Elodea at 15 cm. Record the light intensity at the test tube using a light meter (see fig. 2.22).
4. Allow five minutes for the Elodea to **equilibrate** to the new conditions.
5. Measure the rate of photosynthesis by counting the number of bubbles of oxygen gas produced per unit time (usually five minutes).
6. Record the result, repeat the count and calculate an average.
7. Move the lamp to new positions (30 cm, 45 cm and 60 cm). Repeat steps 3 to 6.
8. Draw a graph of the rate of bubble production against light intensity. Put light intensity on the horizontal axis.

Expected results

The rate of photosynthesis (number of bubbles of oxygen produced per minute) increases as light intensity increases. At the highest light intensities, the rate of photosynthesis may level off due to enzyme saturation.

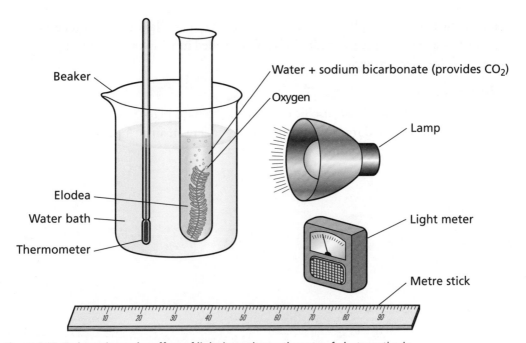

Figure 2.22 To investigate the effect of light intensity on the rate of photosynthesis

Important points to remember

- **Independent or manipulated variable** = light intensity.
- **Dependent variable** = rate of photosynthesis (measured by recording the number of bubbles of oxygen produced per unit time).
- **Controlled variables:**
  - (i) **Temperature:** Using a water bath and thermometer.
  - (ii) **CO_2 concentration:** Using a saturated solution of sodium bicarbonate.

Greenhouse cultivation

The knowledge we have of the requirements and optimal conditions for photosynthesis gave rise to the development of greenhouses for certain types of crop. A greenhouse can artificially control:

- light type and intensity
- temperature
- carbon dioxide concentrations and mineral levels.

This helps protect the crop and ensures maximum productivity.

Light

Light is probably the most important factor affecting photosynthesis. Small increases in light intensity can sharply increase the rate of photosynthesis. In the greenhouse, light can be provided for longer periods artificially. It is important to provide light of the correct wavelengths in greenhouses to maximise photosynthesis.

Temperature

All metabolic reactions in plants are controlled by enzymes. Plant enzymes generally function best at a temperature of 20–25 °C. Controlled heating can ensure an optimum temperature for plant growth.

Carbon dioxide

The levels of CO_2 in the air can also be controlled. Tomato plant yields can be increased if the CO_2 levels are raised from the normal 0.03 per cent in air to 1 per cent in the atmosphere inside the greenhouse.

2016 Q11 (b) HIGHER LEVEL

11. (b) Answer the following questions from your knowledge of photosynthesis.

    (i)   Where in plant cells does the process take place?

    (ii) Name a substance which absorbs light energy for the process.

    (iii) In which pathway of the light stage is oxygen produced?

    (iv) Outline how this oxygen is produced.

    (v) Give **one** fate of this oxygen.

    (vi) What is the fate of the carbon in the carbon dioxide used in the dark stage?

   (vii) Give **one** reason why a suitable temperature is necessary for the dark stage to occur.

  (viii) Aquatic plants such as *Elodea* are particularly suitable for investigating photosynthesis. Suggest a reason for this. **(27)**

LEAVING CERT MARKING SCHEME

11.(b) (i)   *Where:* Chloroplast   **(3)**

    (ii) *Substance:* Chlorophyll   **(3)**

   (iii) *Pathway:* Pathway 2   **(3)**

   (iv) *How O_2 produced:* Water split / using light (energy) **OR** Photolysis / of water   **(2[3])**

    (v) *Fate of O_2:* Released (to the atmosphere) or (used in) respiration **(3)**

   (vi) *Fate of carbon:* Makes carbohydrate (or named carbohydrate) **(3)**

   (vii) *Why suitable temperature:* (Controlled by) enzymes **(3)**

  (viii) *Why Elodea:* Bubbles (of oxygen visible for counting) **(3)**

Respiration

Respiration is the chemical breakdown of food to release energy. Respiration occurs in every cell in the body.

key point

Respiration is a **catabolic** chemical reaction. In the process, complex biomolecules are broken down to simple inorganic molecules, releasing energy.

There are two types of respiration.

- **Aerobic respiration** is the release of energy from food that requires the presence of oxygen.
- **Anaerobic respiration** is the release of energy from food that does not require the presence of oxygen.

Equation of aerobic respiration

Chemical equation

$C_6H_{12}O_6 + 6O_2 \longrightarrow 6CO_2 + 6H_2O + energy$

Word equation

glucose + oxygen $\longrightarrow$ carbon dioxide + water + energy

Equation of anaerobic respiration in plants (Fermentation)

Word equation

glucose $\longrightarrow$ ethanol + carbon dioxide + energy

Biochemistry of cellular respiration

Aerobic cellular respiration occurs in three stages.

1. **Anaerobic glycolysis**: Occurs in the cytoplasm and does not involve oxygen.
2. **Krebs** or **citric acid cycle**: Occurs in the **lumen** of the mitochondrion and oxygen is necessary.
3. **Electron transport chain** or **oxidative phosphorylation**: Occurs on the **cristae** of the mitochondrion and oxygen is necessary.

Anaerobic glycolysis

This is the breakdown of glucose to pyruvic acid, with ATP being produced.

- In plants, if no oxygen is present, the pyruvic acid is converted to **ethyl alcohol** (ethanol) and **carbon dioxide**. This process is called fermentation.
- In the absence of oxygen, animal cells convert the pyruvic acid to **lactic acid**.

Krebs cycle

- If oxygen is present, the pyruvic acid is converted to **acetyl co-enzyme A** (acetyl co A), releasing a molecule of carbon dioxide.
- The acetyl co A enters the lumen of the mitochondrion and then Krebs cycle begins.
- **Hydrogen** (in the form of NADH) and CO_2 are produced.

Electron transport chain

- The products of the Krebs cycle (NADH) enter the cristae of the mitochondria to begin the electron transport chain.
- The hydrogen, electrons and energy stored in NADH are used to produce **ATP**.
- Finally, oxygen combines with hydrogen to produce the waste H_2O.

HL Aerobic respiration is summarised in fig. 2.23.

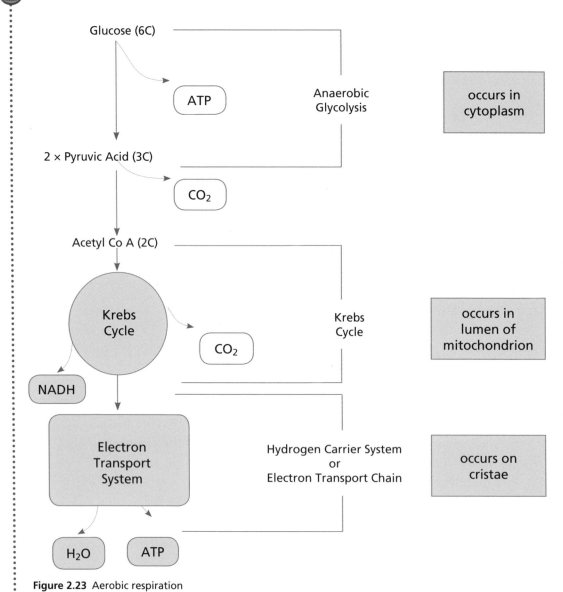

Figure 2.23 Aerobic respiration

Differences between aerobic and anaerobic respiration

Aerobic Respiration	Anaerobic Respiration
Oxygen necessary	Oxygen not necessary
Occurs in mitochondria	Occurs in cytoplasm
Large amount of energy produced	Small amount of energy produced
End products are $CO_2 + H_2O$	End products are lactic acid or ethyl alcohol and CO_2

Mandatory activity

To prepare and show the production of alcohol by yeast

1. Add 250 cm³ of 10 per cent **glucose** to each of two conical flasks.
2. Add 5 g of yeast to one and mix thoroughly.
3. Label the second flask with no yeast 'control'.
4. Add a fermentation lock half-filled with water to both of the flasks (see fig. 2.24).
5. Place both flasks in an incubator at **30 °C** for 24 hours.

To test for alcohol

Test the contents of each flask as follows:

1. Filter the mixture from the conical flask into a beaker.
2. Remove 3 cm³ of the filtrate and place in a test tube.
3. Add 3 cm³ of **potassium iodide** solution.
4. Add 5 cm³ of **sodium hypochlorite** solution.
5. Heat gently for five minutes in a warm water bath.

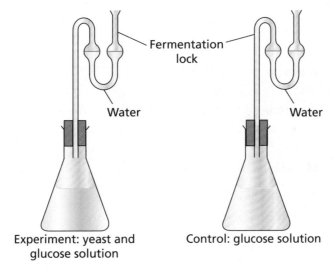

Fermentation lock

Water   Water

Experiment: yeast and   Control: glucose solution
glucose solution

Figure 2.24 Setting up the experiment

Expected results

A positive result for alcohol is the formation of a yellow colour or **yellow crystals**.
A negative result is no yellow colour or crystal formation.

Important points to remember

- The fermentation lock allows gas (carbon dioxide) to escape from the flask but prevents the entry of air or contaminants into the flask. This provides anaerobic conditions.
- The incubator at 30 °C provides the optimum temperature for the yeast cells (enzymes) to respire.
- Substrate = glucose, products = carbon dioxide and ethanol.

2016 Q11 (c) HIGHER LEVEL

11. (c) Answer the following questions from your knowledge of respiration.

    (i) Name the 3-carbon molecule that is an intermediate compound in both aerobic and anaerobic respiration.

    (ii) What name is given to the biochemical pathway by which this intermediate compound is produced?

    (iii) What happens to the intermediate compound referred to in (i) above when oxygen is available and used in the breakdown of glucose? In your answer, refer to:

       1. Krebs cycle.

       2. Electron transport system.

    (iv) What is produced from the intermediate compound referred to in (i) above when oxygen is **not** available

       1. in muscle?

       2. in yeast?   **(24)**

LEAVING CERT MARKING SCHEME

11. (c) (i) *3-carbon intermediate:* *Pyruvate **or** *pyruvic acid   **(3)**

    (ii) *Pathway:* *Glycolysis   **(3)**

    (iii) *Oxidative fate of pyruvate:* Converted to Acetyl (Co- Enzyme A) or enters mitochondrion   **(3)**

       1. or Kreb's cycle: CO_2 produced / ATP produced / NADH produced **(3)**

       2. or electron transport system: protons (or H^+ ions) combine with O_2 or electrons (e^-) combine with O_2 / to form water / energy to ADP and P / to make ATP   **(3)**

       Any one further point from 1 or from 2.   **(3)**

    (iv) 1. *Anaerobic product in muscle:* *Lactic acid or *lactate   **(3)**

       2. *Anaerobic product in yeast:* *Ethanol (and carbon dioxide)   **(3)**

2.3 Cell Continuity

Cell division

Cell division is essential to all living things.
- It allows a multicellular organism to replace worn or damaged cells.
- It is also the basis of reproduction in every organism.

Chromosomes, made up of DNA and protein, carry the genetic code in the nucleus from one generation to the next. In any one individual it is vital that this genetic code is copied faithfully from one cell generation to the next. This is what is known as **cell continuity**.

Haploid and diploid cells

A **haploid cell** has half the full complement of chromosomes (n). The chromosomes do not exist in pairs. Haploid cells are usually either spores or gametes produced during **sexual reproduction**.

A **diploid cell** has the full complement of chromosomes (2n) existing in pairs. All somatic cells (body cells not involved in reproduction) are diploid.

Mitosis

Mitosis is a form of cell division where one cell divides to form two cells, each identical to the parent cell. Mitosis occurs in somatic cells (cells not involved in reproduction).

Significance of mitosis

- In multicellular organisms, genes are faithfully transmitted from one cell generation to the next.
- Unicellular organisms use mitosis for reproduction to produce genetically identical offspring.

Stages of mitosis

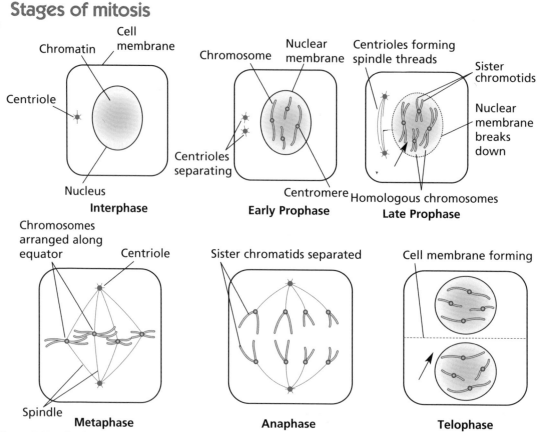

Figure 2.25 Mitosis in a cell with a diploid chromosome number = 4

Interphase

This is a stage between cell divisions when the cell carries out normal activities.

To prepare for cell division at the end of interphase:

- The cell builds up a store of energy.
- Nuclear material (to build new chromosomes) replicates.
- Cell organelles replicate.

The chromosomes are not yet individually visible and form a mass of **chromatin**.

Prophase

- Chromosomes thicken and become visible.
- Homologous chromosomes lie together in pairs.

- Each chromosome forms an identical copy of itself and is joined to the original at the centromere. The pair are called sister chromatids.
- The centriole replicates and they move to opposite sides of the cell.
- The centrioles leave a trail of spindle threads.
- Finally, the nuclear membrane breaks down.

Metaphase

- The chromosomes (sister chromatids) lie in a straight line across the middle of the cell, attached to the spindle threads by the centromere.

Anaphase

- The spindle threads contract, separating the sister chromatids.

Telophase

- A nuclear membrane forms around each set of chromosomes and a cell membrane forms to create two new cells, each with a diploid chromosome number identical to the parent cell.

Cell cycle

This is the sequence of events that occurs between one cell division and the next in mitosis. It can be divided into three main stages:

- In interphase the cell grows and carries out its functions. At the end of interphase the chromosomes replicate, forming sister chromatids. Interphase takes up 90 per cent of the cell cycle.
- Mitosis takes place, forming two new nuclei.
- The cytoplasm finally divides, forming two new daughter cells. The process is called cytokinesis.

Cancer

Cancer is a general term to describe a disorder in the body's growth. Cancer cells fail to respond to normal controls on their multiplication and enlargement. The growth of cancer cells results in a tumour, which crowds out healthy cells. There are two types of tumour. A **benign** tumour grows slowly and the adverse effects are usually to simply apply physical pressure to surrounding tissues. A **malignant** tumour consists of rapidly growing cells that invade and can destroy other tissues. When malignant tumours invade the blood or lymphatic systems, they can spread to other parts of the body.

Lung cancer

Cigarette smoking has been directly linked to lung cancer. Cigarette smoke contains carcinogens, which change or mutate genes that control cell division and development in cells. The most common form of death from cancer in males is lung cancer.

Skin cancer

Skin cancer can be caused by ultraviolet (UV) radiation from sunlight. The UV rays penetrate skin cells, causing mutations in the DNA. With the deterioration of the protective ozone layer, a significant increase in the incidence of skin cancer can be expected.

Meiosis

A second form of **cell division** can occur. It is known as meiosis or reduction division.

> **Meiosis** is cell division where one cell divides to form four cells, each with half the number of chromosomes of the parent cell.

Significance of meiosis

- It is a mechanism of producing gametes (spores in higher plants) with half the number of chromosomes of the parent cell, so at fertilisation the full complement is restored.
- It is a means of producing changes in genotype, leading to **variation** in the offspring.

2.4 Cell Diversity – Tissues, Organs and Systems

When organisms evolved to a multicellular state, their cells became **specialised**. Cells no longer needed to be capable of carrying out all activities to maintain life. Division of labour meant that different cells or groups of cells could carry out specialised functions. Multicellular organisms could organise similar cells into tissues.

Tissues

Examples of **animal tissues** are:

- connective tissue, the skin, for protection
- muscle tissue to move body parts
- nerve tissue for co-ordination.

> A **tissue** is a **group of similar cells** working together. Cells in tissues are more efficient than cells working individually.

Examples of **plant tissues** are:

- xylem tissue, which transports water and provides support
- phloem tissue, which transports dissolved foods.

Organs

- In animals, the heart is an organ made up of muscle, nerve and connective tissues functioning together.
- In plants, the root is an example of a plant organ, containing xylem, phloem and epidermal tissues.

> **Organs** consist of a group of different tissues working together.

Organ systems

The kidney is an organ that works with other organs such as the bladder, renal arteries and veins, and the ureters and urethra. Together, these form the **excretory system**. This system's function is to rid the body of the wastes of metabolism.

The **digestive system** is made up of the gut with accessory organs such as the pancreas and the liver. The digestive system carries out the physical and chemical digestion of food in the body.

Tissue culture

Whole plants can be cultured asexually from very small pieces of tissue extracted from a parent plant. The process can be called **micropropagation**, **tissue culture** or **cloning**. By this process a single plant can produce thousands of genetically identical offspring.

Advantages of tissue culture in plants

- Advantageous genetic characteristics can be faithfully passed to all the offspring.
- Enormous numbers of offspring can be produced.
- The timing of development can be controlled.
- Rare plants can be reproduced easily.

Disadvantages

- All offspring are susceptible to the same diseases and pests, which increases the rates of transmission.
- Long-term micropropagation can lead to plants becoming sterile.

Tissue culture in animals

Tissue culture in animals involves the removal of unspecialised **stem cells** from body tissues or developing embryos. Under the right conditions, in a nutrient solution, these cells can be stimulated to develop into different body tissue cells.

Applications of tissue culture in animals

Tissue culture in animals is used for:

- The development of cells to act as hosts in the culture of viruses to produce viral vaccines.
- The culture of skin tissues to help repair burn injuries.
- The growth of bone tissue used in reconstructive surgery.
- The culturing of organs which will not lead to patient rejection after transplant.

2.5 Genetics

Important definitions

- **Alleles:** Different genes that control the same trait and have the same locus on homologous chromosomes, e.g. T and t.
- **Chromosome:** A threadlike structure in the nucleus, made up of DNA and protein, containing genes.

> **Genetics** is the study of heredity, that is, the transfer of characteristics or traits from one generation to the next. Modern genetics is concerned with the study of genes.

- **Dihybrid cross:** Genetic cross where two characteristics (pairs of genes) are studied, e.g. TtYy × TTYY.
- **Dominant:** The gene that is expressed in the phenotype of the heterozygous condition, e.g. Tt has a tall stem, T is dominant.

- **Fertilisation:** The fusion of two haploid gametes to form a diploid zygote.
- **Gamete:** A haploid sex cell capable of fusion (fertilisation).
- **Genes:** These are units of heredity, made of DNA, that control characteristics in an organism.
- **Genotype:** The genetic make-up of an organism, e.g. Rr.
- **Heterozygous:** An organism that has two different genes controlling the same trait, e.g. Tt.
- **Homozygous:** An organism that has two identical genes controlling the same trait, e.g. TT or tt.
- **Incomplete dominance:** When neither allele is completely expressed in the phenotype of the heterozygous condition, e.g. in cattle the C^R gene codes for red coat, the C^W gene codes for white coat. In the heterozygous condition, $C^R C^W$ codes for roan coat colour.
- **Monohybrid cross:** A genetic cross where only one characteristic or trait (pair of genes) is studied, e.g. Tt × Tt.
- **Phenotype:** Observable characteristics (traits) in an organism, determined by its genes and the genes' interaction with the environment.
- **Recessive:** An allele whose expression in the phenotype is masked by a dominant allele, e.g. Tt has a tall stem, t is recessive.

Gregor Mendel

Mendel was a very careful worker who planned his experiments on a large scale. He recognised that by taking a large number of separate measurements he could eliminate chance effects. He chose the pea plant to study because:

- it had several very sharply contrasting characteristics (for example, short stem, tall stem)
- it did not have intermediate forms (no incomplete dominance).

Mendel's first experiment was to cross a tall-stem (pure breeding – homozygous) pea plant (TT) with a short-stem plant (tt). He gathered the seeds produced and planted them. He then crossed two of the F1 generation (see fig. 2.26).

The **chromosome diagram** shows the location of genes on chromosomes in the nucleus of each plant cell.

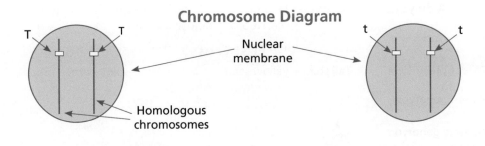

Chromosome Diagram

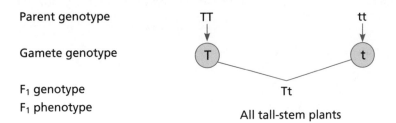

First Cross

Parent genotype	TT	tt
Gamete genotype	T	t
F₁ genotype	Tt	
F₁ phenotype	All tall-stem plants	

Second Cross

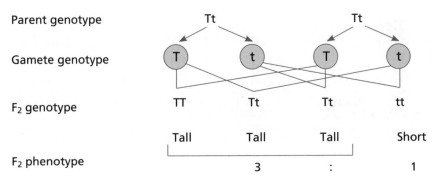

Figure 2.26 Mendel's first experiment

Mendel's Laws

On observation of the results of his first experiment Mendel formed his First Law, the Law of Segregation.

> **Mendel's Law of Segregation:** Traits are controlled by pairs of factors (genes). Only one of any pair can enter a gamete.

Mendel then studied the inheritance of two characteristics at a time. He crossed a plant **homozygously dominant** for two characteristics, tall stem and yellow seeds (TTYY), and a plant **doubly recessive** for the same characteristics (ttyy). He planted the seeds produced and then crossed two of the new offspring (see fig. 2.27).

HL

A **dihybrid cross** between two plants with genotypes of TTYY and ttyy is carried out below:

First Cross

Parent phenotype	Tall stem + yellow seeds Short stem + green seeds
Parent genotype	TTYY × ttyy
Gamete genotype	TY ty
F₁ genotype	TtYy
F₁ phenotype	All offspring have tall stems and produce yellow seeds

Second Cross

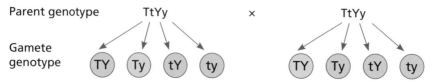

Parent genotype   TtYy   ×   TtYy

Gamete genotype   TY Ty tY ty   TY Ty tY ty

This cross will produce sixteen possible options in the F2 genotype. The easiest way to carry out the cross accurately is to use a Punnet square.

Figure 2.27 Mendel's Law of Independent Assortment

F₂ Genotypes

Gametes	TY	Ty	tY	ty
TY	TTYY	TTYy	TtYY	TtYy
Ty	TTYy	TTyy	TtYy	Ttyy
tY	TtYY	TtYy	ttYY	ttYy
ty	TtYy	Ttyy	ttYy	ttyy

F₂ phenotype
9 Tall + Yellow
3 Tall + Green
3 Short + Yellow
1 Short + Green

From these results, Mendel formulated his second law – the Law of Independent Assortment.

> **Mendel's Law of Independent Assortment:** When gametes are formed, either of a pair of alleles can enter a gamete with either of another pair.

Linkage and the effects on Mendel's Second Law

When Mendel formulated the Law of Independent Assortment, he had studied two traits that were controlled by pairs of genes that were on different homologous pairs of chromosomes.

> Non-allelic genes (genes that control different traits) that are found on the same chromosome are said to be **linked**.

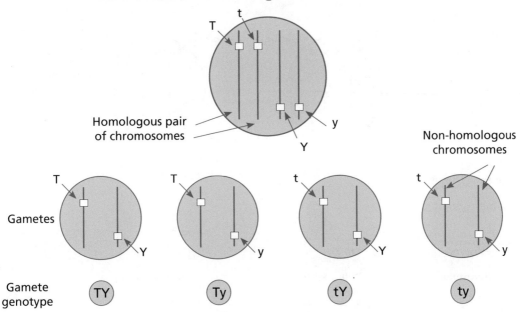

Gametes formed when genes are not linked

Homologous pair of chromosomes

Non-homologous chromosomes

Gametes

Gamete genotype — TY — Ty — tY — ty

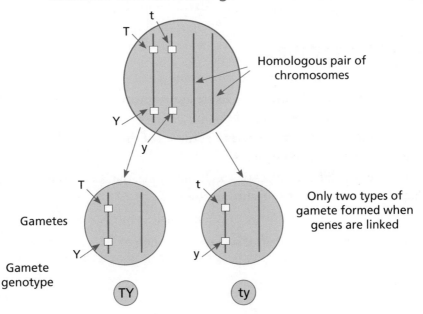

Gametes formed when genes are linked

Homologous pair of chromosomes

Only two types of gamete formed when genes are linked

Gametes

Gamete genotype — TY — ty

Figure 2.28 Linkage

- If the genes were linked, his results would have been different.
- **Linked genes do not follow Mendel's Law of Independent Assortment.** The gametes formed are very different (see fig. 2.28).

Consider the situation if an individual with a genotype TtYy is crossed with an individual with a genotype ttyy and the genes are linked. The chromosome diagrams and the cross are shown in fig. 2.29.

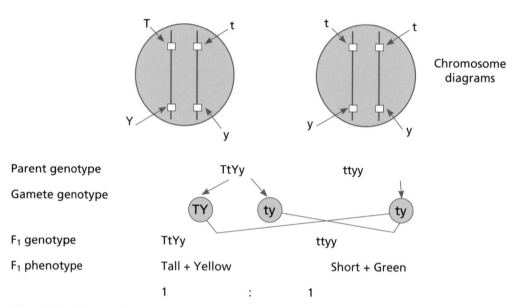

Figure 2.29 Genes are linked

Sex chromosomes

- In humans, the **diploid number** of chromosomes is **23 pairs**.
- Twenty-two pairs of chromosomes are **autosomes** that control almost all characteristics except sex determination.
- One pair of chromosomes determines the sex of the individual and these are known as the **sex chromosomes**.
- There are two different types of sex chromosome, the **X chromosome** (which is the larger of the two) and the **Y chromosome**.
- An individual with a genotype of XX is female, while XY is male.

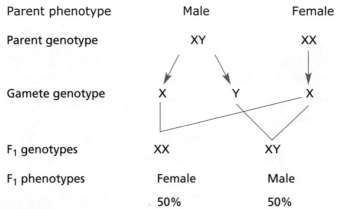

Figure 2.30 Sex determination

Note: The male gamete determines the sex of the child.

Sex linkage

Genes located on the X chromosome that control characteristics other than the sex of the individual are called **sex-linked** genes.

Examples of such genes are the gene for red/green colour blindness and the gene for haemophilia.

Example of sex linkage

In *Drosophila melanogaster* (fruit fly) the gene for eye colour is sex-linked. The gene for red eye, R, is dominant to the gene for white, r. A white-eyed male X_rY is crossed with a heterozygous red-eyed female $X_R X_r$. The genotypes and phenotypes of the offspring produced are shown in fig. 2.31.

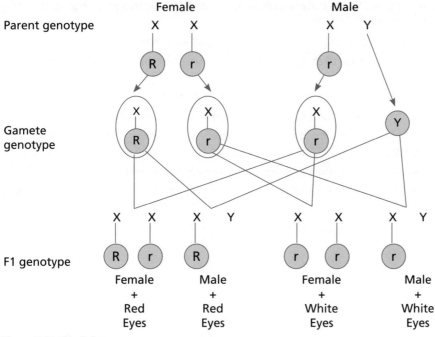

Figure 2.31 Sex linkage

HL

2015 Q10 (a)/(c) HIGHER LEVEL

10. (a) (i) Which famous 19th-century biologist is regarded as 'the father of genetics'?

(ii) In genetics, what is meant by segregation?

(iii) Give an example of a sex-linked characteristic in humans. **(9)**

(c) Unlike the situation in humans, maleness in birds results from the presence of the XX chromosome pair in the fertilised egg and femaleness results from the XY pair. In a particular bird species, green plumage (G) is dominant to yellow plumage (g) and long tail (L) is dominant to short tail (l). The gene for plumage colour is linked to the gene for tail length.

Study the genotypes of the above bird species shown in the diagrams below and in your answer book match the correct genotype to each of the descriptions (i) to (vi). A diagram may match more than one of the descriptions.

(i) A female that is heterozygous in respect of plumage colour and tail length.

(ii) A male that can produce only one type of gamete.

(iii) The individual that can produce the greatest number of different gametes.

(iv) A male, **all** of whose offspring will have long tails.

(v) A female, **all** of whose offspring will have green plumage.

(vi) A male that is homozygous in respect of plumage colour and tail length.

(vii) *In your answer book,* write out the genotypes of the gametes that bird D can produce. **(24)**

LEAVING CERT MARKING SCHEME

10. (a) (i) Mendel   (3)

      (ii) Separation of homologous chromosomes **or** separation of alleles **(3)**

     (iii) Haemophilia **or** (red-green) colour blindness   **(3)**

  (c) (i) *E   **(3)**

     (ii) *C   **(3)**

    (iii) *E   **(3)**

    (iv) *C   **(3)**

    (v) *B   **(3)**

   (vi) *C   **(3)**

  (vii) glX / glY   **(2[3])**

Chromosome and DNA

Definitions

- DNA
- Hydrogen bonds
- Codon
- Triplet code
- Anticodon
- RNA
- Coding and non-coding DNA
- DNA profiling
- Genetic testing and screening
- Genetic engineering
- Transcription
- Translation

Outline

- DNA structure (including diagram)
- Base pairing A-T and C-G
- DNA replication
- RNA and the function of mRNA
- Differences between DNA and RNA
- Protein synthesis (DNA, mRNA, ribosome, triplet code, specific amino acid sequence, correctly folded protein)
- Coding and non-coding DNA
- DNA profiling, stages involved and two applications
- Genetic testing and genetic screening
- Process of genetic engineering and three applications

- Non-nuclear inheritance, i.e. DNA present in mitochondria and chloroplasts
- Detailed structure of DNA including deoxyribose, purine and pyrimidine bases and hydrogen bonds
- Protein synthesis including tRNA and rRNA

Practical Activity

- Isolate DNA from plant tissue

DNA structure

Chromosomes are made up of **deoxyribonucleic acid (DNA)** and **protein**. DNA is the substance that carries the genetic code. It is made up of chains of single units called nucleotides.

A DNA **nucleotide** consists of:

- sugar (deoxyribose)
- phosphate molecule
- nitrogen-containing base.

There are four different types of base:

- **adenine**
- **thymine**
- **cytosine**
- **guanine**

Adenine and guanine are **purine** bases, while thymine and cytosine are **pyrimidine** bases.

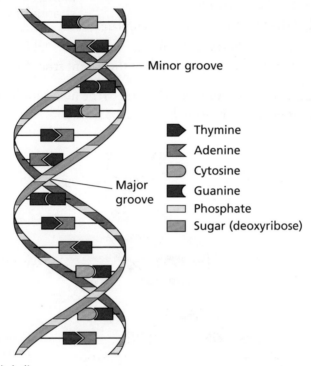

Figure 2.32 DNA double helix

DNA has a **double helix** shape (see fig. 2.32). As you can see from the diagram, it is a ladder-like structure that has been twisted in opposite directions at either end.

- The deoxyribose and the phosphate form the uprights of the ladder and the rungs are pairs of the nitrogen-containing bases.
- The deoxyribose and phosphate strands are **anti-parallel** (run in opposite directions).
- A purine base can only link to a pyrimidine base due to size restrictions. Adenine and thymine can only be paired together, similarly only guanine and cytosine can be paired.
- The base pairs in DNA are held together by hydrogen bonds, which are bonds of electrical attraction.

DNA replication

This is the means by which chromosomes (DNA) can form identical copies of themselves.

DNA replication begins when:

- The **hydrogen bonds** holding the base pairs together break.
- The strands of the parent DNA then separate.
- The DNA double helix unwinds.
- Each strand of the DNA now acts as a template.
- **Nucleotides**, with specific bases from the cytoplasm, match the free bases on each of the parent strands of DNA.

> **key point**
>
> Two enzymes are involved in DNA replication:
>
> 1. **DNA polymerase** creates a new strand of DNA by joining DNA nucleotides together.
>
> 2. **DNA ligase** joins separate strands of DNA together.

This process produces two DNA helices identical to the first. One half of each double helix contains the original parent strand (see fig. 2.33).

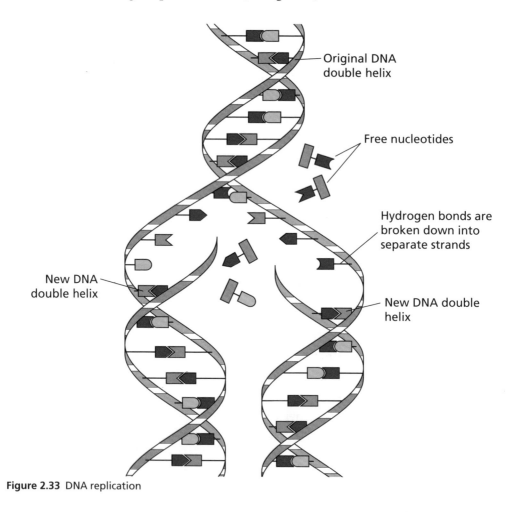

Figure 2.33 DNA replication

DNA and protein synthesis

Specific enzymes control all chemical reactions in the body. Enzymes are proteins made up of a defined sequence of amino acids.

- DNA codes for amino acids, and their correct sequence, through a triplet code.
- The nitrogen-containing bases (A, T, G and C) in DNA are arranged in threes along the double helix.
- Each triplet codes for one specific amino acid.
- DNA sends its code for an enzyme to the ribosome by messenger RNA, or **mRNA**.
- **Ribosomes**, in the cytoplasm, make the proteins.

Protein synthesis

The whole process of protein synthesis occurs in two stages: transcription and translation.

1. Transcription

- When a particular enzyme is needed by a cell, the portion of DNA in the nucleus that codes for it unwinds, exposing its bases.
- A strand of mRNA is produced from RNA nucleotides, mirroring the DNA code.
- When complete, the strand of mRNA separates from the DNA and moves to a ribosome (rRNA) in the cytoplasm.

The nucleotides on mRNA are arranged in a triplet code forming codons. Each **codon** codes for a particular amino acid.

tRNA also has a triplet code of nucleotides that match the codons of mRNA. Each matching triplet is known as an **anticodon**.

2. Translation

- At the ribosome, the mRNA code is matched by nucleotides of transfer RNA (tRNA). Each tRNA molecule carries a specific amino acid.
- The tRNA carries the amino acids in the correct sequence to the ribosome.
- The amino acids are then linked together in strict order, producing the protein (enzyme), which then assumes its unique **folded shape**.

Differences between DNA and RNA

	Structure	Function	Location
DNA	Deoxyribose is the sugar Double helix shape Base pairing Has the base thymine instead of uracil	Codes for genotype	Nucleus
RNA	Ribose is the sugar Single helix No base pairing Has the base uracil instead of thymine	mRNA carries code from nucleus to rRNA (ribosomes); tRNA transports amino acids	Cytoplasm

Non-nuclear inheritance of DNA

Many scientists believe that **mitochondria** and **chloroplasts** evolved from forms of bacteria. Through evolution they became assimilated into larger-celled organisms. The two organisms then formed a mutualistic (symbiotic) relationship, giving rise to plant and animal cells. Mitochondria and chloroplasts are unique as organelles in that they:

Non-nuclear DNA in chloroplasts and mitochondria does not undergo meiosis or fertilisation during sexual reproduction.

- contain their own DNA
- can replicate themselves in the cell.

Mandatory activity

To isolate DNA from plant tissue

Note: *The extra information in brackets below is not required when describing the procedure.*

1. Add 3 g of **salt** to 10 cm³ of washing-up liquid in a beaker and bring up to 100 cm³ with distilled water. (*Salt reduces the attraction between protein and DNA. Washing-up liquid breaks down phospholipid membranes in the cell.*)
2. **Chop** some onion into very small pieces and add to the beaker. (*Chopping breaks down the cell walls and allows cytoplasm to leak out.*)
3. Put the beaker in a water bath at **60 °C for exactly 15 minutes**. (*High temperature denatures enzymes harmful to DNA. Any longer than 15 minutes, the DNA itself would break down.*)
4. **Cool** the mixture by placing in a large beaker of ice water for five minutes. (*Slows the activity of any remaining enzymes harmful to DNA.*)
5. Place the mixture in a **blender for three seconds**. (*Blending further breaks down cell walls and membranes. Any longer than three seconds shreds the DNA.*)
6. **Filter** the mixture into a second beaker. (*Removes cellular debris.*)
7. Place 10 cm³ of the filtrate into a test tube.
8. Add 3 drops of **protease solution** and mix gently. (*Breaks down proteins associated with DNA.*)
9. Trickle 10 cm³ of **ethanol from the freezer** down the side of the test tube.
10. Leave for a few minutes to settle. (*Cold ethanol draws water from DNA, condensing it.*)
11. Gently stir with a glass rod.

Expected result

White mucus-like DNA forms at the interface of the ethanol and the filtrate.

DNA profiling

Humans have 23 pairs of chromosomes in the nucleus of every cell in the body (with the exception of gametes). A single chromosome can have up to 4,000 genes, which code for different traits. It is known that 90 per cent of DNA does not code for any gene or protein in the body.

> **Coding DNA** refers to sections of DNA that make up genes. They code for an enzyme or protein.
>
> **Non-coding DNA** describes sections of DNA, between genes, that do not code for an enzyme or protein. They are often referred to as 'junk DNA'.

The sections of non-coding DNA often have repeating nucleotide sequences in sections called hypervariable regions. The number and length of these nucleotide sequences vary between individuals, but are similar in related individuals.

Forensic scientists use DNA profiling to compare DNA from hair, saliva, blood or semen found at the scene of a crime.

> **DNA profiling or DNA fingerprinting** uses the repeating nucleotide sequences of non-coding DNA to produce a pattern of bands for comparison of individuals.

The procedure for DNA profiling is outlined in fig. 2.34.

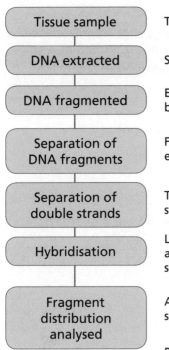

Tissue sample — Tissue sample is obtained from source.

DNA extracted — Solvents used to separate DNA from proteins.

DNA fragmented — Enzymes called restriction endonucleases digest the DNA, breaking it into fragments at specific points.

Separation of DNA fragments — Fragments are separated on the basis of size using gel electrophoresis.

Separation of double strands — The sample is immersed into an alkali to separate DNA into single strands.

Hybridisation — Labelled nucleotide sequences of specific code, called probes, are added. These match certain parts of the core nucleotide sequences and pair up with them.

Fragment distribution analysed — An X-ray film is placed over the nucleotides and the marked sections with the probes appear as dark bands.

Patterns of banding from different samples are compared.

Figure 2.34 DNA profiling

Applications of DNA profiling

DNA profiling can be used to:

- prove the parentage of a child
- detect criminals guilty of violent crimes
- confirm pedigree in animals.

Genetic screening and testing

> **Genetic screening** is the use of laboratory procedures to test a large number of individuals to identify those who may have or may pass on a genetic disorder.

Example: Amniocentesis is the testing of the cells in the amniotic fluid around the foetus for genetic disorders such as **Down's syndrome**.

> **Genetic testing** describes the laboratory procedures used to investigate an individual suspected of having a high risk of a genetic disorder, based on family history or a positive screening test.

Example: The testing for the genetic disorder responsible for **cystic fibrosis**.

Genetic engineering and applications

> **Genetic engineering** is a process where genes from one organism are introduced into the genome (DNA) of an unrelated organism, usually micro-organisms.
>
> The micro-organisms with the new genes are replicated and used to create large quantities of useful chemicals.

Note: The process is often referred to as **recombinant DNA technology**.

Genetic engineering involves the following steps.

- Locating a specific gene in a donor cell.
- Isolation of the gene.
- Insertion of the gene into the DNA that has been removed from a micro-organism.
- Transferring the DNA and new gene back into the micro-organism.
- Replicating the micro-organism and harvesting the chemicals produced due to the new gene.

The process is summarised in fig. 2.35.

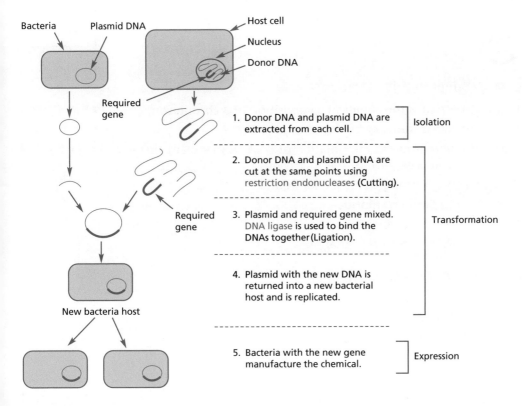

Figure 2.35 Genetic engineering

Applications of genetic engineering

- There is enormous demand for the hormone insulin to treat **insulin-dependent diabetes**. This disease used to be treated by using insulin obtained from the pancreas of cattle and pigs. Subtle differences in the forms of insulin stimulated antibody responses in some humans. Genetic engineering is now used to isolate the human gene for insulin production. The gene is inserted into a host bacterium to produce large quantities of human insulin.
- Genetically modified **plants** have an advantageous gene inserted into their DNA which is passed on to future generations. Characteristics such as disease and insect resistance have been introduced into food crops. The improved plant has greater yields.
- In **animals**, genetic engineering has been used to increase meat and milk yields in cattle.
- In **microorganisms**, bacteriophage can be genetically engineered to kill antibiotic-resistant bacteria.

7. (a) (i) What is the chemical composition of a chromosome?

(ii) What is meant by the term *junk DNA*?

(b) (i) In relation to the isolation of DNA from a plant tissue, explain why you used each of the following:

1. Washing-up or similar liquid.

2. Sodium chloride.

3. Protease.

4. Freezer-cold ethanol.

LEAVING CERT MARKING SCHEME

7. (a) 5 + 1

(a) (i) DNA and protein

(ii) Non-coding (DNA)

(b) 8 + 8 + 1 + 1

(b) (i) 1. To breakdown the (cell) membrane(s)

2. To cause the DNA to clump

3. To breakdown (or remove or digest) the protein in the chromosomes

4. To bring the DNA out of solution **or** to make the DNA visible **or** to separate the DNA

10. (b) Write notes on each of the following topics in relation to nucleic acids. In each case your notes should contain three points. Do not give diagrams in your answers.

(i) Complementary base pairs.

(ii) Codons.

(iii) Transcription. (27)

LEAVING CERT MARKING SCHEME

10. (b) (i) (Two bases joined by) hydrogen bonds / purine with pyrimidine / Cytosine with Guanine / Adenine with Thymine in DNA / Adenine with Uracil in RNA **or** Thymine replaced by Uracil in RNA (3[3])

(ii) Sequence(c) of three bases / on DNA / on mRNA **or** on tRNA / (each codon) codes for one amino acid / that codes for a start (or stop) (3[3])

(iii) mRNA is formed / using a (single) strand of DNA / (DNA acts) as a template (or described) / in nucleus / (catalysed by) RNA polymerase (3[3])

Evolution

A fossil is the remains of a once-living plant or animal.

Evolution is a process where organisms that now exist have descended from different ancestors. It is brought about by mutations (genetic changes). Improved characteristics are then passed on to offspring by **natural selection**.

Natural selection (Darwin and Wallace)

Darwin and **Wallace** developed the theory of natural selection, based on their observations, to explain the process of evolution.

Their observations included the following:

- Organisms generally produce large numbers of offspring.
- Population numbers tend to remain constant as survival rates are low.
- Variation occurs between individual members of any species.

Natural selection is the way in which organisms become better adapted to their environment due to a **mutation**.

- The genes for the improved characteristics can then be passed on to their offspring.
- Natural selection is thought to play a large role in the process of evolution.

key point

Inherited variations are the basis of natural selection and evolution.

Variation in a species over long periods can give rise to new species. This process is known as **speciation**.

Evidence for evolution

There are different sources of evidence that support the theory of evolution. One source is the study of comparative anatomy.

Comparative anatomy

This is a comparison of bone structure in the forelimb of very diverse animals such as the whale, mole, bat and human. They all have a **pentadactyl limb** arrangement of bones (see fig. 2.36).

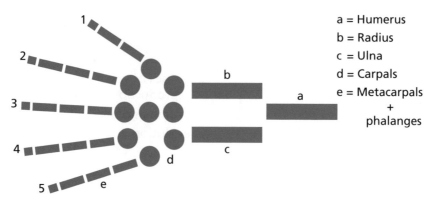

a = Humerus
b = Radius
c = Ulna
d = Carpals
e = Metacarpals
+
phalanges

Figure 2.36 Pentadactyl limb

key point

- Limbs of various animals that have the same basic structure but different functions are known as **homologous structures**.
- Different functions for limbs with similar structures are examples of **adaptative radiation**.

Variation of species

A **species** is defined as a group of similar individuals of common ancestry that can interbreed to produce fertile offspring.

Different characteristics found in the individuals of a species are described as **variations**.

Variations can occur due to:
- the shuffling of genes that occurs, during meiosis, to produce gametes
- mutations.

Mutations

A **mutation** is a change in the nucleotide sequence of DNA that can alter the genotype of an organism.
Mutations are inherited if they are present in a gamete.

Causes: Mutations can occur with exposure to mutagens such as X-rays, radioactivity and chemicals called carcinogens.

Gene and chromosome mutations

A gene mutation is caused by a change in the base (nucleotide) sequence of the DNA in a gene. This can alter the protein it produces.

Example: Cystic fibrosis is caused by a gene mutation.

A chromosome mutation is due to a change in a **chromosome** structure or a change in the number of chromosomes present in an organism.

Example: Down's syndrome is caused by the presence of an extra chromosome.

2016 Q14 (a) HIGHER LEVEL

14. Answer any two of (a), (b), (c). (30, 30)

(a) (i) Explain the term *species*.

(ii) What term is used to describe the differences which exist between individuals of a species?

(iii) The differences referred to in (ii) form the basis of evolution by natural selection.

1. Explain the term *evolution*?

2. Outline the role of natural selection in evolution.

(iv) Explain the term *mutation*.

(v) Give **one** example **each** of a disorder caused by:

1. Gene mutation.

2. Chromosome mutation.

(vi) Give **one** cause of the differences referred to in (ii) above, other than mutation.

LEAVING CERT MARKING SCHEME

14. (a) (i) *Species*: A group of organisms capable of interbreeding to produce fertile offspring. **(3)**

(ii) Intraspecific differences: *Variation **(3)**

(iii) 1. *Evolution*: Genetic changes (in populations) / in response to environment / over time / giving rise to new species **(2[3]3)**

2. *Role of natural selection*: Better adapted survive / reproduce / adaptation is inherited / adaptation (becomes) more common **(2[3])**

(iv) *Mutation*: A change in DNA (or gene **or** chromosome **or** genetic material) **(3)**

(v) 1. *Gene mutation disorder*: Sickle cell anaemia **or** any valid example **(3)**

2. *Chromosome mutation disorder*: Down's syndrome **or** any valid example **(3)**

(vi) *Cause of variation*: Sexual reproduction **or** meiosis **or** formation of gametes **or** fertilisation of gametes **or** independent assortment **(3)**

2012 Q6 HIGHER LEVEL

6. (a) In genetics, what is meant by the term *variation*?

(b) Variation can result from mutation. Name **one** other cause of variation.

(c) Name **two** types of mutation.

(d) Name **two** agents responsible for increased rates of mutation.

(e) Briefly explain the significance of mutation in relation to natural selection.

LEAVING CERT MARKING SCHEME

6. 2(7) + 6(1)

(a) Differences (within a population or within a species or between individuals)

(b) Sexual reproduction **or** meiosis **or** independent assortment **or** environmental

(c) (i) Gene (mutation)

(ii) Chromosome (mutation)

(d) (i) Example 1

(ii) Example 2

(e) New phenotypes **or** new types **or** new features / Better adapted **or** survival of the fittest (or advantageous) **or** less well adapted (or disadvantageous)

UNIT 3

The Organism

3.1 Diversity of Organisms and Classification

There is an enormous variety of living things in the biosphere. To simplify the study of these different organisms, we try to classify them into groups. The groupings are based on internal and external features. Most classification systems reflect the evolutionary relationships between organisms. Marguilis and Schwartz produced the most recent **five kingdom classification**.

Kingdom	Characteristics	Examples
1. Prokaryotes	1. No membrane-bound organelles	Bacteria, cyanobacteria
2. Fungi	1. Eukaryotic 2. Non-cellulose cell wall 3. Non-photosynthetic, absorb food through hyphae 4. Produce spores	Moulds, mushrooms, yeasts
3. Protoctists	1. Eukaryotic 2. Most are unicellular	Protozoa (amoeba), algae (fucus)
4. Plants	1. Eukaryotic 2. Cell wall of cellulose 3. Photosynthetic 4. Multicellular	Liverworts, mosses, ferns, conifers, angiosperms
5. Animals	1. Eukaryotic 2. Non-photosynthetic 3. Nervous system 4. Multicellular	Platyhelminthes, nematodes, annelids, molluscs, arthropods, echinoderms, chordates

Bacteria (Monera)

Bacteria are micro-organisms found everywhere (ubiquitous). They are neither plants nor animals, as they do not have a membrane-bound nucleus. Bacteria are known as prokaryotic organisms. They are much smaller in size than either plant or animal cells. Bacteria are classified according to their shape:

(a) **Coccus** are round.

(b) **Rods** are cylindrical.

(c) **Spirals** have random shapes.

A generalised bacterium is shown in fig. 3.1.

Bacteria can also be classified as:

(a) **Aerobic**: require oxygen to live.

(b) **Anaerobic**: do not require oxygen.

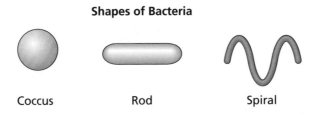

Shapes of Bacteria

Coccus   Rod   Spiral

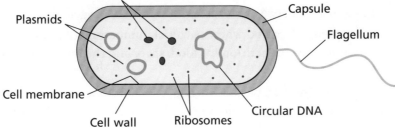

Generalised Structure of a Bacterium

Food reserves

Plasmids

Capsule

Flagellum

Cell membrane

Cell wall   Ribosomes   Circular DNA

Figure 3.1 Bacteria

Reproduction and growth curves of micro-organisms

Bacteria reproduce asexually by **binary fission**. One mature cell divides to form two identical daughter cells. Reproduction can occur as often as once every 20 minutes under suitable conditions. The growth rate of a colony of bacteria can be represented by a growth curve. Different rates of growth in numbers are observed over time (see fig. 3.2).

HL

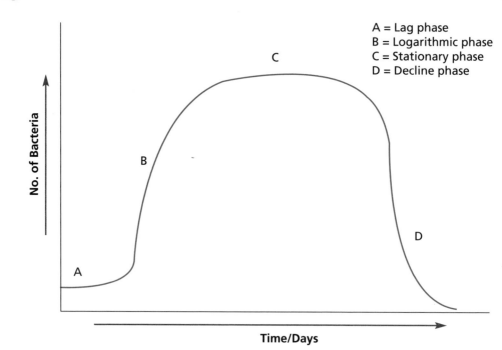

Figure 3.2 Growth curve of micro-organisms

A = Lag phase
B = Logarithmic phase
C = Stationary phase
D = Decline phase

Stages of a growth curve

- **The lag phase**: A slow rate of reproduction, as the bacteria have only started to grow and a period of time is necessary for adaptation to the new environment.
- **The logarithmic phase**: A rapid growth in numbers as the bacteria reproduce rapidly, due to an abundance of resources such as food, oxygen, space, etc.
- **The stationary phase**: A period where bacterial numbers neither increase nor decrease. This is due to competition for food, space and the build-up of toxic wastes.
- **The decline phase**: The final period where bacterial numbers decline due to the increased competition for space and food and the build-up of toxic wastes.

Growth Phases in Bioreactors

The growth curve shown in fig. 3.2 represents the growth phases of micro-organisms that would exist in a bioreactor during the processing of a **batch culture** of product.

A **continuous flow culture**, in a bioreactor, would maintain the micro-organisms at the logarithmic phase.

Factors affecting the growth of bacteria

- **Temperature:** Metabolism is controlled by enzymes which are sensitive to temperature.
  In general, a temperature of 30 °C to 40 °C is optimal.
- **Food:** An abundant source of nutrition is vital for rapid growth.
- **Oxygen** (if the bacteria are aerobic).
- **pH:** Most bacterial enzymes work optimally at a pH range close to 7.
- An **absence of competition** and **toxins or wastes**.

Endospores

- Some bacteria have the ability to form **resistant, thick-walled spores** to survive unfavourable conditions.
- These spores are known as **endospores** and can endure very harsh environments for many years in this state.
- When favourable conditions return, the endospore absorbs water, which weakens the thick outer wall. The bacterium then divides by binary fission, returning to its normal state.

Nutrition in bacteria

Since bacteria can be found anywhere in the biosphere, they must be able to gain nutrition in many different ways. Fig. 3.3 summarises the types of nutrition in bacteria.

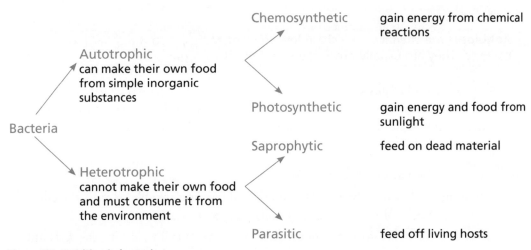

Figure 3.3 Nutrition in bacteria

- **Chemosynthetic** bacteria are involved in many parts of the **nitrogen cycle**. These and other bacteria are very important in the recycling process of minerals, which is vital for all living things.

- **Photosynthetic** bacteria such as cyanophytes use sunlight to make food. These are vital in nature as they often form the first stages of freshwater and marine food chains.

- **Saprophytic** bacteria include *Pseudomonas* which break down the remains of dead plants and animals to ammonia. Saprophytic bacteria play an essential role in recycling the materials of dead organisms.

- **Parasitic** bacteria cause diseases such as tuberculosis and cholera. Parasitic bacteria play an important role in nature, causing disease and death, which acts as a form of population control.

> **key point**
>
> Humus in soil is formed by saprophytic bacterial activity. It is the remains of organic matter undergoing further decomposition. Humus is a vital component of fertile soil. It improves drainage, aeration, mineral and water retention.

Economic importance of bacteria

Beneficial

- The bacteria *Streptococcus* is used in yoghurt-making.
- *Streptomyces* is cultured to make antibiotics.

Harmful

- Tuberculosis in cattle is caused by *Mycobacterium*.
- Cholera is caused by the bacteria *Vibrio*.

Antibiotics

> **Antibiotics** are chemicals which, in low concentrations, stop the growth of bacteria. They are usually produced by other micro-organisms.

Antibiotics are powerful weapons against infectious diseases caused by pathogenic bacteria. Penicillin was the first antibiotic to be produced in large quantities. Its use saved many injured casualties in the Normandy battles of 1944. Today there are over fifty different antibiotics used in medicine.

Antibiotic resistance in bacteria

- Sometimes a few members of a population of bacteria are able to resist the effects of an antibiotic. This resistance is usually due to a mutation.
- Excessive use of an antibiotic removes non-resistant strains, leaving the resistant bacteria to flourish. New, more powerful antibiotics must then be developed.
- Intensive farming of chickens and pigs often involves the addition of small quantities of antibiotics to the animal feed. This has produced healthier animals that grow more quickly. Unfortunately, widespread use facilitates the development

of resistant strains of bacteria. The residues of the antibiotics are then consumed by humans, assisting the development of more antibiotic-resistant bacteria.

MRSA

MRSA is a multi-antibiotic-resistant bacterium capable of causing life-threatening disease. Overcrowding of patients and poor hygiene control has seen the establishment of this pathogen in some Irish hospital wards. Further studies have shown that MRSA spreads rapidly in populations when:

- there is a tendency to overprescribe antibiotics
- widespread use of broad-spectrum antibiotics occurs.

Fungi

Fungi are eukaryotic, heterotrophic micro-organisms. Their cell walls are made of **chitin**. Many fungi have their cells arranged in a network of threads called **hyphae**.

Saprophytic fungi break down the remains of dead plants and animals. In the soil they play an essential role in recycling the materials of dead organisms. Humus in soil is formed by such activity.

key point

- A common edible fungus is the mushroom.
- Toadstools are examples of poisonous fungi.

Parasitic fungi

Parasitic fungi can cause disease in animals and plants.

- In plants, an example of a parasitic fungus is **potato blight**.
- **Athelete's foot**, in humans, is caused by a parasitic fungus.

Saprophytic fungi

There are two types of saprophytic fungi studied.

1. *Rhizopus* (bread mould): A multicellular, saprophytic fungus with aseptate hyphae.
2. *Saccharomyces* (yeast): A unicellular saprophytic fungus.

Rhizopus (bread mould)

Rhizopus is a saprophytic multicellular fungus. It is **aseptate**, i.e. it does not have cross walls separating its cytoplasm into separate cells (see fig. 3.4).

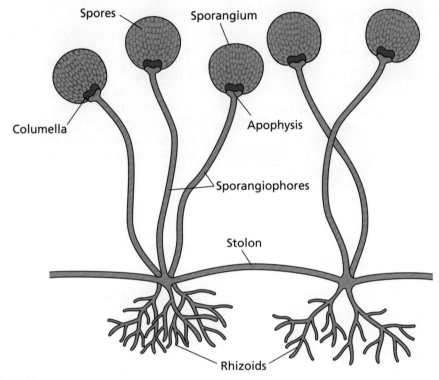

Figure 3.4 *Rhizopus*

Life cycle

There are two forms of reproduction: asexual and sexual.

Asexual reproduction

- *Rhizopus* reproduces asexually by producing spores in sporangia.
- Under dry conditions the spores are released and spread by the air.
- Spores can then germinate to produce new hyphae.

Sexual reproduction

- Sexual reproduction occurs when the hyphae of two different strains of *Rhizopus* come in contact with one another.
- Outgrowths occur on the hyphae, forming gametangia.
- The gametangia fuse, forming a thick-walled, diploid zygospore.
- Under suitable conditions the zygospore germinates to produce a sporangium.
- Finally, the sporangium bursts when mature, releasing spores (see fig. 3.5).

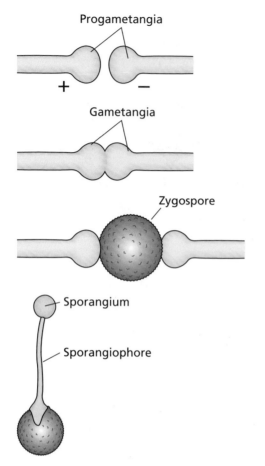

Progametangia

1. Hyphae of different strains of Rhizopus grow toward one another.

Gametangia

2. The hyphae form gametangia at their tips.

Zygospore

3. A thick-walled zygospore is formed around the zygote. It is then released.

Sporangium

Sporangiophore

4. Under suitable conditions the zygospore germinates, forming a sporangiophore and sporangium.

Figure 3.5 Sexual reproduction in *rhizopus*

Nutrition

- The hyphae secrete digestive enzymes onto the substrate on which they grow.
- The enzymes **externally digest** any carbohydrates, lipids or proteins present.
- The products of digestion are then absorbed into the hyphae.

Saccharomyces (yeast)

Saccharomyces is a saprophytic, unicellular fungus (see fig. 3.6).

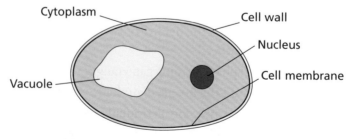

Cytoplasm

Cell wall

Nucleus

Cell membrane

Vacuole

Figure 3.6 *Saccharomyces* – adult yeast cell

Reproduction

Saccharomyces reproduces asexually in a process called **budding**.

- A mature cell nucleus divides by **mitosis** to produce two new nuclei.
- The nuclei separate as a new cell is formed, budding out of the parent (see fig. 3.7).

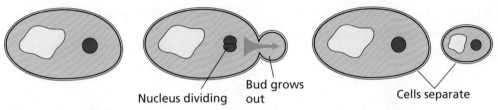

Nucleus dividing   Bud grows out   Cells separate

Figure 3.7 *Saccharomyces* – asexual reproduction (budding)

Economic importance of fungi

Beneficial

- Yeast is used in the brewing industry, converting carbohydrate to alcohol.
- The carbon dioxide produced during the respiration of yeast causes dough to rise in the baking industry.

Harmful

- Potato blight is caused by the fungus *Phytophera*. Heavy infection destroys crop yields.
- The fungus *Merulius* causes dry rot in wood.

Laboratory procedures when culturing micro-organisms

The culturing of bacteria and fungi is essential for the study of micro-organisms.

> **Asepsis** or **aseptic technique** describes a series of steps to ensure the absence of unwanted micro-organisms.
>
> The term **sterile** describes an object or environment free of contaminating micro-organisms.

Aseptic technique

A. Preparation of the medium

1. Boil some agar, peptone and water in a beaker.
2. Pour the mixture into boiling tubes.
3. Sterilise the tubes and agar in a pressure cooker.
4. Tighten the lids on the boiling tubes when cool and store in a fridge.

B. Pouring agar plates

1. Loosen the caps on the boiling tubes and place in boiling water to melt the nutrient agar.
2. Remove the cap of the boiling tube and flame its mouth in a Bunsen burner (*to prevent contamination*).
3. Remove the lid of a sterile Petri dish, holding it just above the base.
4. Quickly pouring the agar, replace the lid and swirl gently to spread evenly.
5. Leave to set for five minutes (see fig. 3.8a).

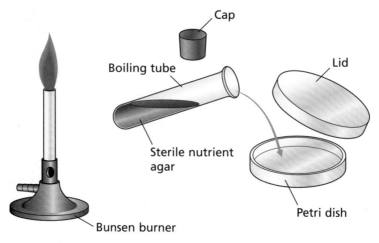

Figure 3.8a Pouring agar plates

C. Inoculation of agar plates

1. Heat an **inoculating loop** in a Bunsen flame (*to sterilise it*).
2. Touch the loop at the edge of the agar, away from the source of micro-organisms to cool it and then pick up some living cells.
3. Remove the lid of a sterile Petri dish, holding it just above the base.
4. Streak the agar with the inoculating loop to inoculate the Petri dish.
5. Replace the lid, seal and label (see fig. 3.8b).

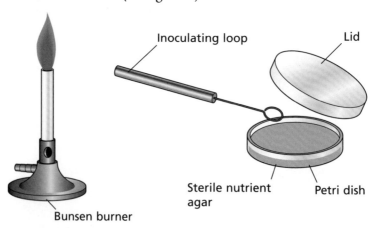

Figure 3.8b Inoculation of agar plates

D. Incubation of agar plates

1. Store the plates upside down in an incubator. (*This prevents an evaporation condensation cycle, which would increase the possibility of contamination.*)
2. Set the temperature at 37 °C for three days. (*This is to promote the growth and reproduction of each organism to form visible colonies.*)

Precautions for the examination of agar plates

The following precautions are necessary in case pathogens have been cultured on the agar plates.

- All micro-organisms must be treated as if harmful to humans.
- The plates should be sterilised with a few drops of strong disinfectant 24 hours before inspection.
- The plates should never be opened for inspection.

Identification of micro-organisms

- **Fungi** are seen as black or white, threadlike or furry growths.
- **Bacteria** are seen in colonies as small, shiny pinheads.

Use of a control

In all experiments, a **control** is used as a comparison and as a test of the validity of the results. A Petri dish of sterile nutrient agar is always poured and incubated with the other Petri dishes. This is called the control and is not inoculated with any micro-organisms. If the culturing technique is good, there will be no colonies of micro-organisms on the control.

Disposal

All Petri dishes and reusable equipment must be sterilised in a pressure cooker at high pressure before disposal or storage.

Mandatory activity

To investigate the growth of leaf yeast using agar plates and controls

Note: *The extra information in brackets below is not required when describing the procedure.*

1. Selecting an **ash tree**, collect some leaves using **sterile gloves** and place into a sterile plastic bag. (*This reduces the possibility of contamination.*)
2. Swab down the bench with disinfectant.
3. Seal and label one unopened **malt agar** plate to act as a **control**.
4. Flame the **cork borer** with a Bunsen burner (*to sterilise it*) and allow it to cool.
5. Use the cork borer to remove five discs from the ash leaves.
6. Invert a second malt agar plate. Remove the base (with the agar) and place face down on the bench. (*This reduces the possibility of contamination from the air.*)

7. Flame the forceps (*to sterilise it*) and allow to cool.

8. Using the forceps, smear five portions of **petroleum jelly** onto the lid of the agar plate.

9. Reflame the forceps and cool.

10. Use the forceps to attach the five discs of ash leaves to the petroleum jelly, making sure the lower epidermis of each is exposed. (*Most fungi grow on the underside of the leaves.*)

11. Replace the lid, seal and label the dish.

12. Leave the dish with the discs uppermost over the malt agar for 24 hours. (*This allows fungal spore to fall from the leaf onto the malt agar.*) See fig. 3.9a.

13. Turn the dish upside down and leave for a further three days in an incubator at 20 °C. See fig. 3.9b.

14. Compare this dish with the control (set up in step 3).

15. After the experiment, sterilise all the apparatus in a pressure cooker before disposal.

Figure 3.9a and 3.9b Using agar plates

Expected results

Leaf yeasts appear as pink colonies. The number of yeast colonies on each dish is recorded.

Note: An abundance of pink colonies is an indicator of the absence of pollutants in the air.

2016 Q3 HIGHER LEVEL

3. The diagram shows asexual reproduction in yeast.

   (a) How do you know from the diagram that the reproduction is asexual?

   (b) What name is given to this type of asexual reproduction?

   (c) (i) How does the genetic make-up of the new yeast cell relate to that of the parent cell?

   (ii) Explain your answer.

   (d) Give an advantage and a disadvantage of asexual reproduction in organisms such as yeast.

   (e) Name another organism which belongs to the same kingdom as yeast.

LEAVING CERT MARKING SCHEME

3. 2(5) + 5(2)

(a) *Why asexual*: Only one parent (cell)

(b) *Asexual reproduction in yeast*: Budding

(c) (i) *Genetic make-up compared to parent*: Identical

(ii) *Explain*: (Reproduced by) mitosis

(d) *Advantage*: Rapid **or** characteristics maintained (or example) **or** no variation

Disadvantage: Increased risk of disease **or** overcrowding **or** increased competition **or** no variation

(e) *Same kingdom as yeast*: Rhizopus **or** (field) mushroom **or** named fungus **or** name fungal group

2015 Q15 (c) HIGHER LEVEL

15. (c) (i) Name the **three** general shapes of bacterial cells.

(ii) What is meant by the term *pathogen*?

(iii) What is the difference between 'aspesis' and 'sterility'?

(iv) Give one way in which bacterial cope with unfavourable environments.

(v) When growing bacteria in the laboratory, samples are taken regularly from the growth medium and the number of cells per millilitre is counted. A graph of the results is drawn and is similar to the one shown below.

Answer the following questions in relation to this graph.

1. Name the stages B, C and D.

2. Explain what is happening during stage C.

3. Distinguish between batch processing and continuous flow in food processing. Refer to the stages labelled in the graph in your answer.

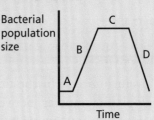

Bacterial population size / Time

LEAVING CERT MARKING SCHEME

15. (c) (i) Rod (**or** bacilli) / spherical (**or** cocci) / spiral (**or** spirilla)   **(3[1])**

(ii) Disease-causing (agent or organism)   **(3)**

(iii) Asepsis: Free of pathogens   **(3)**

Sterility: Free of (micro)organisms   **(3)**

(iv) (Endo)spore formation   **(3)**

(v) 1. B = *log(phase)   **(1)**

C = *stationary (phase)   **(1)**

D = *decline (or *death) (phase)   **(1)**

2. Limited space (or food or O_2) **or** waste (or toxin) accumulating **or** death rate = birth rate   **(3)**

3. *Batch processing*: Fixed amount of nutrients added at beginning **or** (bioreactor) emptied at end of production   **(3)**

Continuous flow: Nutrients continuously fed into (bioreactor) **or** product removed continuously **(3)**

Stage Reference:

Batch: All stages occur

OR **(3)**

Continuous flow: Stage B (or C) (or log or stationary phase) maintained

Protista (amoeba)

All the organisms in this group are eukaryotic and most are **unicellular**. Amoeba is an example of a unicellular animal in this group. Amoeba has heterotrophic nutrition.

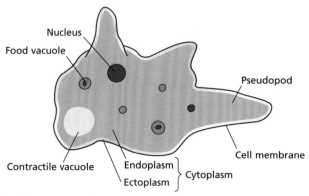

Figure 3.10 Protoctista, e.g. amoeba

Movement

Movement occurs by the alternation of the outer ectoplasm (clear) and inner endoplasm (granular) between plasmagel (solid) and plasmasol (liquid) states. These changes cause streaming in the cytoplasm and the formation of **pseudopods** (see fig. 3.10).

Reproduction

Reproduction is asexual. A single cell divides by **mitosis** to produce two new identical daughter cells. This is referred to as **binary fission**.

Contractile vacuole

Water constantly enters the cell by osmosis. Energy (ATP) is necessary to pump it out against the diffusion gradient. The water is gathered in the contractile vacuole and it is pumped outside the cell using energy (active transport).

key point

Marine (sea-living) amoebae do not have the need for a contractile vacuole, as their cytoplasm is isotonic with the sea water and excess water does not diffuse into the cell.

Monocots and dicots

There are two main types of flowering plants:

- Monocotyledons
- Dicotyledons

Differences between Monocotyledons and Dicotyledons

Monocots	Dicots
1. Seeds contain a single cotyledon	1. Seeds contain two cotyledons
2. Fibrous root system	2. Tap root system
3. Herbaceous (non-woody) plant	3. Woody plant
4. Flower parts in threes	4. Floral parts in fours or fives
5. Leaves narrow with parallel veins	5. Netted pattern of leaf veins
6. Vascular bundles are scattered in stem	6. Vascular bundles in rings in stem

Flowering plants can be divided into two main regions:

1. Root system
2. Shoot system

System	Functions
Root system	1. Absorbs water and minerals from soil
	2. Anchors the plant
	3. Sometimes stores food
Shoot system	1. Stem supports leaves and flowers
	2. Stem transports food, water and minerals
	3. Leaves make food (photosynthesis)
	4. Leaves carry out gaseous exchange
	5. Flowers carry out reproduction

Plant tissues

Plant tissues can be divided into four main types.

1. **Dermal tissue**, which covers and protects the plant from water loss and the entry of disease.

    Example: Epidermis (see fig. 3.11).

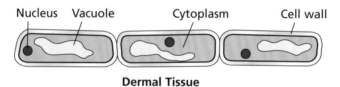

Dermal Tissue

Figure 3.11 Plant tissues: Epidermis

2. **Ground tissue**, which has a packing and storage function.

    Example: Parenchyma in cortex (see fig. 3.12).

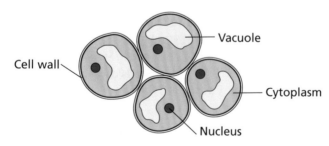

Ground Tissue (Parenchyma)

Figure 3.12 Plant tissues: Cortex

3. **Meristematic tissue** is responsible for new growth and cell division (mitosis).
4. **Vascular tissue** is involved in the transport of food, water and minerals around the plant.

    Example: xylem and phloem (see fig. 3.13).

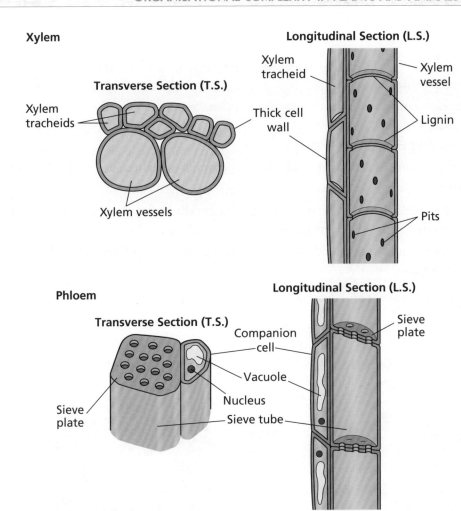

Figure 3.13 Vascular tissue

Xylem tissue
Structure: Dead, lignified with thick cell wall.
Function: Transport of water and minerals.
Location: Vascular bundles and any vascular tissue.

Phloem tissue
Structure: Living, thin-walled cells.
Function: Transport of food and hormones.
Location: Vascular bundles.

Meristematic tissue (Meristems)
Structure: Living, thin-walled cells.
Function: Cell division and growth.
Location: Shoot and root tips and cambium.

Plant growth

In general, there are two types of growth in plants:

1. **Primary thickening**

   The **elongation** of shoot and root tips by primary meristematic tissue dividing by mitosis.

2. **Secondary thickening**

   The **widening** of the shoots and roots by secondary meristematic tissue dividing by mitosis.

   - It occurs when the meristematic cambium cells in the vascular bundles divide by mitosis to produce new phloem to the outside and new xylem to the inside.
   - This process is repeated every year, causing the widening and strengthening of the stem.

Diagrams of monocot and dicot stems and roots are seen in fig. 3.14a and 3.14b.

Monocot and dicot stems

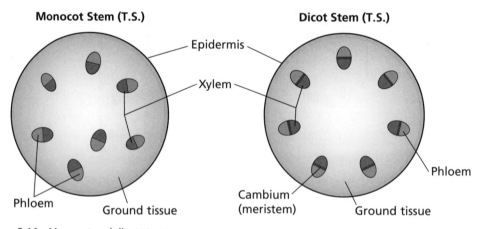

Figure 3.14a Monocot and dicot stems

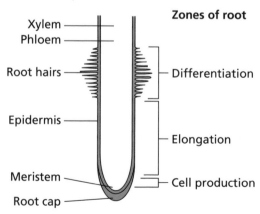

Figure 3.14b Dicot root (L.S.)

Dicot roots

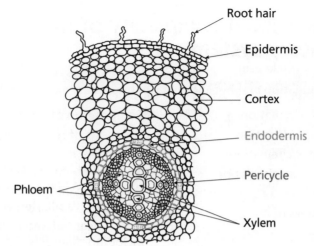

Root hair
Epidermis
Cortex
Endodermis
Pericycle
Phloem
Xylem

Figure 3.14c Dicot root (T.S.)

Mandatory activity

To examine microscopically the transverse section of a dicot stem

1. Place a buttercup stem in a cut-out potato to provide support.
2. Use a **wet, backed blade** to cut **very thin** sections from an internode section of the stem.
   (Safety: Always cut away from your fingers)
3. Place a drop of water on a glass slide, and with a **paint brush** gently place a cutting onto the drop, preventing the formation of any air bubbles.
4. Add a few drops of toluidine blue stain and leave for one minute.
5. Rinse off excess stain gently using dripping water from a tap.
6. Place a cover slip, **at an angle**, over the sample very carefully to prevent the formation of air bubbles.
7. Examine under low and high power with a light microscope.
8. Draw labelled diagrams of the images produced.

Expected result

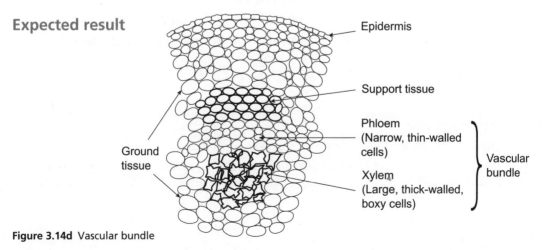

Epidermis
Support tissue
Phloem
(Narrow, thin-walled cells)
Ground tissue
Xylem
(Large, thick-walled, boxy cells)
Vascular bundle

Figure 3.14d Vascular bundle

Organisational complexity of the human circulatory system

Definitions
- Closed circulation
- Double circulation
- Systemic circulation
- Pulmonary circulation
- Plasma
- Pacemaker
- Artery
- Vein
- Capillary

Outline
- Composition of blood (cells and plasma)
- Functions of red, white blood cells and platelets
- Haemoglobin in red cells
- Different types of blood vessels (arteries, arterioles, capillaries, venules, veins)
- Differences between arteries and veins including diagrams
- Labelled diagram of the heart
- Main blood vessels to and from the heart
- Coronary arteries and veins
- Mechanism of heartbeat
- Pulse
- Blood pressure
- Hepatic portal system
- Blood groups (A, B, AB and O) and Rhesus factor
- Effects of smoking and diet on the heart
- ECF (tissue fluid) and how it is formed
- Lymphatic system (lymph nodes and lymph vessels)
- Three functions of the lymphatic system

- Detailed structure of red and white blood cells
- Types of white blood cells (lymphocytes and monocytes)
- Control of heartbeat (SA and AV nodes)
- Heart cycle (systole and diastole periods)

Practical Activities
- Dissect, display and identify an ox's or a sheep's heart
- Investigate the effect of exercise on the breathing rate or pulse of a human

Very small animals do not need a system of circulation. They can rely on passive diffusion for their oxygen supplies from their environment. Factors such as animal size, shape and activity determine the need for a circulatory system. Humans have a well-developed circulatory system. It has the following features.

- It is a **closed system**, which means the blood is contained in a continuous system of blood vessels.
- There is a muscular heart, made up of specialised **cardiac muscle**, pumping the blood under high pressure.
- It is a **double circulation system** consisting of two separate circulations (shown in fig. 3.15):

 (i) A pulmonary circulation, from the heart to the lungs and back again.

 (ii) A systemic circulation, from the heart to the body and back again.

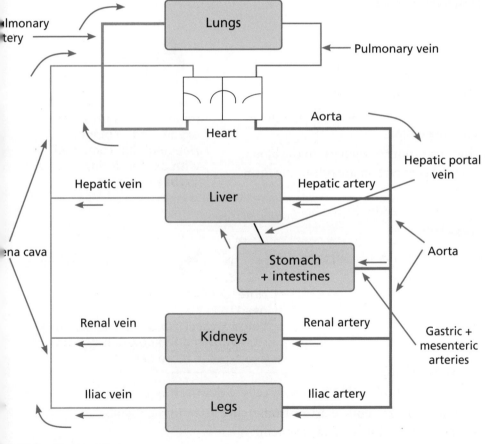

3.15 Double circulation

In humans, the blood consists of two main components, **cells** and **plasma**. Plasma is 90 per cent water, which contains dissolved food, wastes and blood proteins.

The different constituents of blood can be seen in fig. 3.16.

Constituents of blood

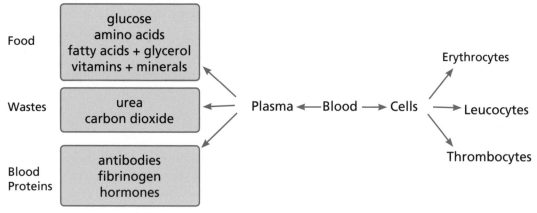

Figure 3.16 Constituents of blood

Blood cells

Erythrocytes (Red blood cells)

Structure: They have a biconcave shape and have neither a nucleus nor mitochondria. They contain the protein haemoglobin.

Function: They **transport oxygen** gas in the blood. They can also transport carbon dioxide in the form of carbonic acid.

Source: They are produced in the red bone marrow of large bones.

Leucocytes (White blood cells)

There are two main types:

- lymphocytes
- monocytes

Note: Ordinary level students only need to know the composition of blood and cell functions. Higher level students need to know cell structures and types in more detail.

Lymphocytes

Structure: Have a nucleus.

Function: Produce **antibodies** that help body cells to destroy foreign objects.

Source: Produced in the red bone marrow from stem cells or in the thymus. All lymphocytes operate from the lymphatic system.

Monocytes

Structure: Large white blood cells with a nucleus.

Function: Leave the blood circulation by amoeboid movement to **engulf foreign matter**.

Source: Produced from stem cells in the red bone marrow.

Thrombocytes (Platelets)

Structure: No nucleus, very small.

Function: Blood clotting.

Source: Produced in the red bone marrow.

Blood groups

In humans there are four blood groups.

- A
- B
- AB
- O

Blood group is determined by the presence or absence of two types of protein on the surface of the red blood cells. These are called the A and B antigens.

Another protein that may be present on the red blood cells of an individual is the **Rhesus factor**. A person with the factor is described as Rhesus positive. Individuals without the factor are Rhesus negative.

Knowledge of blood group and the presence or absence of Rhesus factor is essential to avoid complications in blood transfusions.

Blood vessels

There are three main types of blood vessel: arteries, veins and capillaries.

Arteries

- Carry blood away from the heart.
- They have a thick muscle layer to help prevent over-expansion during heartbeat.
- Usually carry oxygenated blood.
- Have a small lumen but no valves.

Arterioles are small arteries carrying blood from larger arteries to capillaries.

Veins

- Carry blood to the heart.
- They have a thin muscle layer.
- Usually carry deoxygenated blood.
- They have a large lumen and have valves. Valves prevent the backflow of blood.

Venules are small veins carrying blood away from capillaries to veins.

Capillaries

- Very small vessels, the walls being only one cell thick.
- They allow dissolved substances to enter and leave the blood by diffusion and through intercellular spaces.
- Are in close contact with tissue cells.

The heart

- The heart is made up of a specialised muscle called cardiac muscle. It is different to other muscles in that it does not fatigue or 'tire'.
- The heart consists of four chambers, a left and right **atrium** as well as a left and right **ventricle**.
- The **tricuspid valve** on the right side and the **bicuspid valve** on the left side separate the atria from the ventricles.
- The **septum** separates the left side of heart from the right side.
- The **left ventricle** of the heart is more muscular than the right as it is required to produce sufficient force to pump blood all round the body.
- **Semilunar valves** prevent the backflow of blood once pumped out of the ventricles (see fig. 3.17).

> **key point**
>
> The semi-lunar valves prevent blood from flowing back into the heart during diastole.

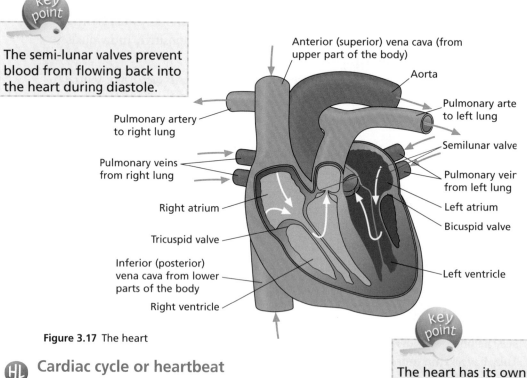

Anterior (superior) vena cava (from upper part of the body)

Aorta

Pulmonary artery to right lung

Pulmonary arte to left lung

Semilunar valve

Pulmonary veins from right lung

Pulmonary veir from left lung

Right atrium

Left atrium

Tricuspid valve

Bicuspid valve

Inferior (posterior) vena cava from lower parts of the body

Left ventricle

Right ventricle

Figure 3.17 The heart

Cardiac cycle or heartbeat

- The cycle begins with the atria in relaxed mode (**diastole**).
- Blood fills both atria from veins and the AV valves (bicuspid and tricuspid) remain closed.
- As the pressure rises, the AV valves open, allowing blood to fill both ventricles.
- Both atria then contract (**systole**).
- Both ventricles then contract when full, closing the AV valves.
- Blood is pushed out through arteries and the cycle begins again.

> **key point**
>
> The heart has its own blood supply, provided by the **coronary arteries**. They bring oxygenated blood from the base of the aorta to all of the heart muscle. Coronary veins bring blood away from heart tissue.

Pulse

The pulse is caused by the wave of blood being forced through the arteries when the ventricles contract. It can be felt in the body where arteries are near the skin. Pulse rate is a measure of heartbeat rate. It is often measured at the wrist, where the arteries are close to the skin.

Blood supply to the heart

- Some of the oxygenated blood leaving the left ventricle is passed to the openings of three coronary arteries, located just above the semi-lunar valve.
- The coronary arteries supply the thick heart muscle with blood rich in oxygen and nutrients.
- Deoxygenated blood is collected by the coronary veins, which drain into the right atrium.

Control of heartbeat

- The **pacemaker** (SA Node) triggers heartbeat. It is located in the wall of the right atrium. It stimulates both atria to contract simultaneously.
- This contraction stimulates a second knot of muscle, the AV Node. It is located between the atria and the ventricles. The impulse is spread along the septum, causing the ventricles to contract.

Factors affecting the rate of heartbeat

Exercise, emotional disturbance and age all affect the rate of heartbeat.

- Stimulants increase the rate of heartbeat, e.g. alcohol and adrenaline. Depressants reduce the rate of heartbeat, e.g. sleeping pills.

Mandatory activity

To dissect, display and identify an ox or sheep heart

Note: *The extra information in brackets below is not required when describing the procedure.*

1. Place the heart on a dissecting board, front upwards. (*This is done by looking for the coronary artery at the front, which extends from the top right side diagonally down to the bottom left.*)
2. Locate the two atria on top and the two ventricles below.
3. Identify the pulmonary artery and the aorta on top. (*The aorta has a much thicker wall.*)
4. Make a sketch of the external structure of the heart.
5. Make two shallow cuts on each side of the heart (see fig. 3.18a).
6. Observe the bicuspid valve (*two flaps*) on the left side and the tricuspid valve (*three flaps*) on the right side of the heart.
7. Using a probe, trace out the chordae tendinae from the papillary muscle to the valves.
8. Cut back the aorta to locate the semi-lunar valve (*three half-moon-shaped flaps*).

9. Find the two openings of the coronary arteries just above the semi-lunar valves at the base of the aorta.

10. Trace the coronary artery using a seeker.

11. Flag and label all the parts and sketch the internal structure of the heart.

12. Wash and sterilise all instruments after use.

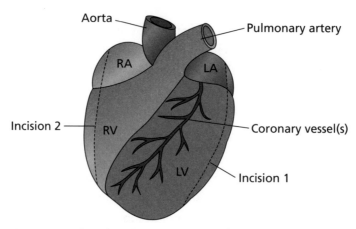

Figure 3.18a Dissecting an ox or sheep heart

Mandatory activity

To investigate the effect of exercise on the pulse rate of a human

1. Locate your pulse at the wrist or temple. Use your index finger to measure the pulse (see fig. 3.18b).

2. Sit relaxed on a chair for five minutes.

3. Count the number of pulses per minute.

4. Repeat twice, calculate the average and record. (*This is the heart's resting rate.*)

5. Walk gently for five minutes. Immediately measure and record the pulse rate.

6. Walk briskly for five minutes. Immediately measure and record the pulse rate.

7. Run for five minutes. Immediately measure and record the pulse rate. Repeat and calculate the average rate.

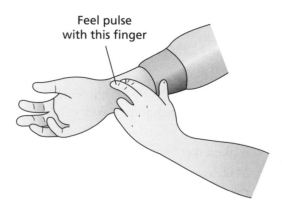

Feel pulse with this finger

Figure 3.18b Pulse

8. Compare the different pulse rates.

9. Draw a bar chart of the results.

Expected results

The pulse rate increases with the intensity of exercise. After resting, the pulse rate will gradually return to normal as CO_2 levels in the blood decrease.

Blood pressure

Blood pressure is a measure of the force exerted by the blood as it is pumped through the closed system of blood vessels in the body.

The higher the pressure, the more strain that is experienced by the heart. Blood pressure is controlled by:

- the regulation of the rate of heartbeat
- the control of the diameter of arterioles supplying blood to capillaries.

Heart disease

Three major factors in heart disease are:

- Smoking
- Poor diet
- Lack of exercise

Smoking

Smoking can cause heartbeat and blood pressure to increase, straining the heart. Nicotine and carbon monoxide in cigarette smoke can interfere with heartbeat and may cause the heart to stop beating. Heavy cigarette smoking causes atherosclerosis, a disease where the arterial walls thicken. Fatty deposits build up, forming raised patches on the inside of the arteries. These restrict blood flow and increase the risk of internal blood clotting.

Poor diet

Large amounts of animal fats in the diet raises the cholesterol levels in the blood. High cholesterol levels cause atherosclerosis, which increases the strain on the heart.

Lack of exercise

Regular exercise leads to a healthy circulation. It reduces blood pressure by improving blood flow through arterioles. Exercise increases the capacity of the heart to pump blood, which reduces the rate of heartbeat.

Lymphatic system

Blood in capillaries is under pressure and leakage of plasma and its dissolved substances occurs, forming extracellular fluid (ECF). All tissue cells are bathed in this fluid and it facilitates the diffusion of materials between the blood and the cells. Excess ECF must be returned to the blood. This occurs by:

- draining back into the bloodstream at the venous end of the capillary (lowest pressure)
- entering the lymphatic system through small tubes called lymph capillaries (see fig. 3.19).

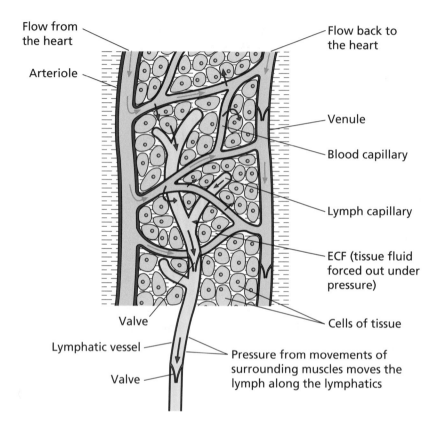

Figure 3.19 Tissue, blood and lymphatic systems

The fluid that enters the lymph capillaries is called lymph. Lymph capillaries drain into larger vessels called lymphatic vessels. The lymphatic vessels have valves to prevent the backflow of lymph.

key point

Skeletal muscles involved in movement in the body provide the pressure to push lymph along the lymphatics.

Functions of the lymphatic system

- Return lost fluids from the blood vessels to the blood.
- Detect and fight disease.
- Transport digested lipids and fat-soluble vitamins around the body.

key point

Lymph nodes are swellings along the lymph vessels where the lymph is filtered. They are a source of **lymphocytes** which in turn produce antibodies against disease.

exam Q

2016 Q8 HIGHER LEVEL

HL

8. (a) Answer the following questions in relation to the human pulse.
   (i) What is the pulse?
   (ii) What makes the wrist (or temple, or neck) a suitable part of the body to detect a pulse?

(b) Answer the following questions in relation to the investigation you carried out on the effect of exercise on the breathing rate or pulse rate.
   (i) What was the control in this investigation?
   (ii) What is the purpose of this control?
   (iii) You carried out this investigation on two women of the same age. One of the women (A) was a very fit athlete. The other (B) was overweight and rarely took exercise.
   1. Appropriately label each of the axes below.
   2. Draw two curves or plots to summarise the most likely results of your investigation, clearly labelling which curve relates to which individual.

   (iv) Recovery time is the duration of the period following exercise during which the breathing rate or pulse rate returns to normal. Suggest how you might measure recovery time.

LEAVING CERT MARKING SCHEME

8. (a) 2(3)
   (i) *Pulse*: The (rhythmic) stretching (or expanding or vibrating) of an artery
   (ii) *Why pulse at wrist*: Artery near the surface

(b) 4(4) + 4(2)
   (i) *Control*: Rate (measured) at rest
   (ii) *Purpose of control*: To compare with the results (of the experiment)
   (iii) *Axes labels* x-axis 'duration (of exercise)' or 'time' or level of exercise
   y-axis 'rate'
   Curve or plot showing: B increases by a greater amount

(iv) *How measure recovery time*: Immediately (after exercise) / count pulse or breathing / rate or per minute / measure length of time until rest rate reached **Any three**

2014 Q3 HIGHER LEVEL

3. The diagram shows a region of tissue that includes body cells and parts of the circulatory and lymphatic systems.

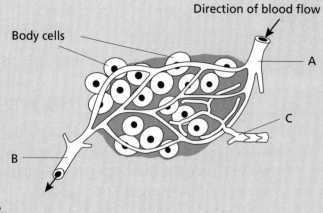

Direction of blood flow

Body cells

A

C

B

(a) Name part C.

(b) What type of blood vessel is A?

(c) If a transverse section of A were viewed under the microscope, state one way in which it would differ from a transverse section through B.

(d) Give two functions of the lymphatic system.

(e) Give one way in which lymph differs from blood.

(f) Name a major blood vessel that returns the blood in B to the heart.

LEAVING CERT MARKING SCHEME

3. 8 + 7 + 5(1)

(a) C = Lymph vessel

(b) Arteriole [*accept* artery]

(c) Narrow(er) lumen **or** thick(er) wall **or** no valves

(d) Maintains a constant level of ECF **or** drains fluid or returns fluid to blood / manufacture of lymphocytes **or** maturation of lymphocytes / filtering bacteria / fighting infection / transport of named material

(e) No red blood cells **or** no haemoglobin / no platelets / no clotting (proteins) / higher fat level [*accept* correct colour difference]

(f) Vena cava

Nutrition in the flowering plant

Definitions
- Osmosis
- Root pressure
- Diffusion
- Transpiration
- Transpiration stream
- Translocation
- Perennation

Outline
- The uptake and transport through the plant of
  - Water
  - Minerals
  - Carbon dioxide
  - Carbohydrate
- Labelled diagrams of one example of modifications for food storage in the
  - Root
  - Stem
  - Leaf
- Cohesion tension model of water transport   HL

Nutrition in flowering plants can be considered under three headings.
- The uptake and transport of water and minerals.
- The absorption and use of carbon dioxide.
- The formation and transport of carbohydrates.

The uptake and transport of water and minerals

Water enters the roots, by osmosis, through root hairs.

The mechanisms by which water is transported across the root to the xylem vessels are:
- Osmosis from cell to cell through the cytoplasm and vacuoles of cortex cells. This force, due to osmosis, exerts a push from the root upwards and is known as root pressure.

key point

Root hairs are tiny extensions of root epidermal cells. They increase the surface area for absorption. The root hairs are adapted to their function by the absence of a cuticle, which would prevent the entry of water.

- Diffusion through the spaces between cell walls. This pathway is thought to account for up to 90 per cent of water transport across the root.

HL Dixon and Joly proposed that the main influence in the transport of water and minerals up the stem is a suction force developed by the transpiration of water vapour through the stomata in the leaves.

Their **cohesion-tension model** of xylem transport proposed that:

- Transpiration draws water up the xylem vessels in the stem.
- The cohesion forces of water molecules in the narrow xylem vessels are so strong that they can support a column of water up to 80 metres in height.
- The constant transpiration pull from the leaves allows for a constant flow of water from the root hairs across the root to the xylem vessels.

Minerals

- Minerals dissolved in the soil water are transported into the plant along the same pathway as water.
- Minerals are essential to the manufacture of all the **proteins, lipids and carbohydrates** necessary for a healthy plant.
- The **endodermal cells** (endodermis) in the root are surrounded by an impermeable layer called the Casparian strip. All water and minerals must pass through the cytoplasm of the cells at this point (see fig. 3.20).

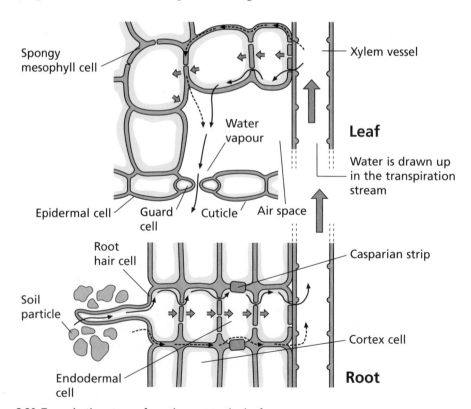

Figure 3.20 Transpiration stream from the root to the leaf

The absorption and use of carbon dioxide

Carbon dioxide is produced by all cells in the plant through **respiration**. This can be used for the process of photosynthesis if required.

If more CO_2 is necessary, gaseous exchange with the atmosphere must occur. Most gaseous exchange occurs through pores in the leaves called **stomata**. Guard cells control the size of stomata. In general, the stomata are opened wide in daylight when CO_2 is required for photosynthesis (see fig. 3.21).

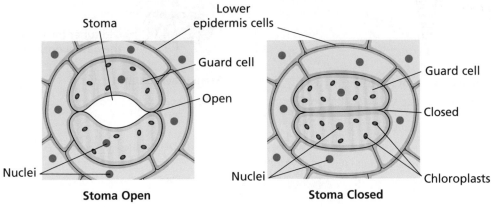

Figure 3.21 Stoma and guard cells observed from below the leaf

The formation and transport of carbohydrates

Carbohydrate is manufactured in the process of photosynthesis. Carbohydrate is transported from the leaves, around the plant, in the form of **sucrose**. The transport of carbohydrate around the plant is known as **translocation**. Translocation occurs through the phloem sieve tubes and companion cells.

Modified plant food storage organs

Many plants require the ability to store food from one growing season to the next in order to complete their life cycle. This process is known as **perennation**. Food storage can occur in the modified organs of the root, stem or leaves (see fig. 3.22).

Organ	Modified Structure	Example
Root	Tap root	Carrot
Stem	Underground stem or tubers	Potato
Leaf	Bulb	Onion

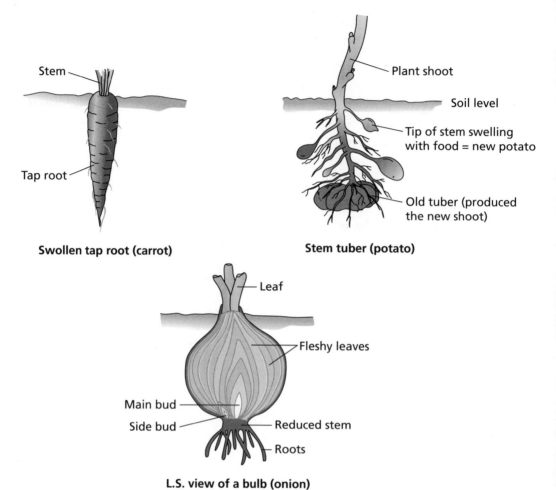

Swollen tap root (carrot)

Stem tuber (potato)

L.S. view of a bulb (onion)

Figure 3.22 Modified organs of the root, stem and leaves

Nutrition in the human

Definitions
- Herbivore
- Carnivore
- Omnivore
- Ingestion
- Digestion
- Absorption
- Assimilation
- Egestion
- Peristalsis
- Mechanical digestion
- Chemical digestion

Outline
- Basic structure of the alimentary canal
- Dentition and human dental formula
- Location, action and products of amylase, lipase and pepsin
- Role of symbiotic bacteria in the digestive tract
- Benefits of fibre
- Adaptations of small and large intestines in relation to their function
- Structure and diagram of villus with blood vessels
- Transport of the products of digestion into the blood and lymphatic system
- Hepatic portal system
- Functions of the liver
- Functions of bile
- Balanced diet

Animals have heterotrophic nutrition, i.e. they must capture and consume their food such as plants or other animals. Animals can be classified according to their diet.

- **Herbivore:** An animal that feeds on plants only, e.g. rabbit, sheep.
- **Carnivore:** An animal that feeds on other animals only, e.g. cat, hedgehog.
- **Omnivore:** An animal that feeds on both plants and animals, e.g. pig, human.

Stages of nutrition

Respiration is a vital process for life and it is carried out in all living cells. Food is essential for respiration, and for food to get to all the cells of a multicellular animal, it must go through the following stages:

- **Ingestion:** The taking in of food to the body through the mouth.
- **Digestion:** The mechanical and chemical breakdown of food.
- **Absorption:** The products of digestion are passed into the blood for transport. Absorption occurs through the processes of osmosis, diffusion and active transport.
- **Assimilation:** The movement of digested food from the blood into the cells.
- **Egestion:** The unused, unabsorbed remains of food passed out of the body.

The digestive system

The human digestive system consists of a number of organs that:

- Mechanically digest food by tearing and crushing food into smaller pieces, e.g. mouth and stomach.

- Secrete digestive juices to chemically digest and dissolve food, e.g. duodenum.
- Provide large vascularised (many blood vessels) surface areas to absorb the products of digestion into the blood, e.g. ileum.
- Reabsorb water and concentrate unused remains for egestion, e.g. large intestine (see fig. 3.23).

The alimentary canal is a term used to describe the continuous tube that extends from the mouth to the anus. It consists of the following regions: mouth, oesophagus, stomach, duodenum, ileum, colon, rectum and anus. The walls of the alimentary canal contain circular and longitudinal muscles that gradually contract and relax to push food along its length.

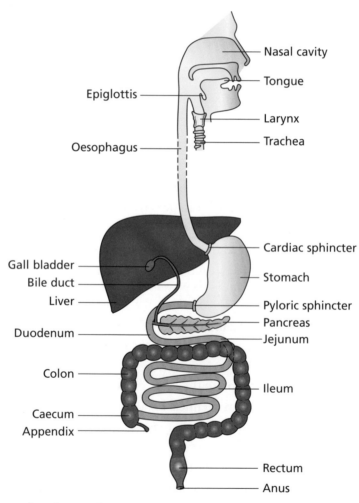

Figure 3.23 Human alimentary canal

Mechanical digestion begins with the tearing and crushing action of the teeth in the mouth. The process is continued in the stomach, where the stomach muscles gradually contract and relax to further crush the food until it has a liquid consistency.

> **Peristalsis** is the involuntary muscular contractions of the circular and longitudinal muscles that push food through the alimentary canal.

Chemical digestion is carried out by enzymes that break the large food biomolecules down to single units so they can be absorbed into the blood.

Teeth and dentition

Teeth play a vital role in **mechanical digestion**. They crush and tear food, softening it by mixing with saliva. A tooth is a hard structure embedded in the jawbone and adapted to cutting and grinding food.

Dentition

Dentition describes the type and arrangement of teeth in the jaws. The diet of any animal can be determined by an examination of its teeth.

There are four different types of teeth which have different locations and functions in the jaw. These are:

- **Incisors** and **canines** at the front of the jaw, used for gripping, cutting and tearing food.
- **Premolars** and **molars** at the back, for crushing and grinding food.

Dental formula

> The **dental formula** describes the number and type of teeth in one-half of the complete upper and lower jaws.

The human (omnivore) dental formula is given in the table below.

Human	Incisor	Canine	Premolar	Molar
Upper jaw	2	1	2	3
Lower jaw	2	1	2	3

Small intestine and adaptations to its functions

The small intestine is almost 8 metres long. It consists of the duodenum, jejunum and the ileum. The duodenum provides secretions from three sources.

- Bile from the gall bladder.
- Pancreatic juices from the pancreas.
- Digestive juices from the walls of the duodenum.

The ileum is the longest part of the small intestine. The main function of the ileum is the absorption of the products of digestion.

Adaptations of the small intestine to its functions

- It is very long, and its inner lining has finger-like projections called villi that increase the surface area (see fig. 3.24).
- The surface of each villus has smaller projections called microvilli.
- The blood capillaries are just below the surface to facilitate absorption.
- Cells at the surface have mitochondria, providing energy for active transport.
- Secretory cells produce large amounts of watery secretions with digestive enzymes.

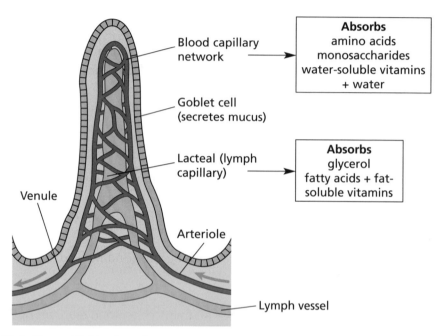

Figure 3.24 A villus and its blood supply

Secretions and digestive enzymes in the alimentary canal

Site of Production	Secretion	Enzyme	Environment pH	Substrate	Products
Salivary Gland (Mouth)	Saliva	Amylase	pH = 8 (alkaline)	Starch	Maltose
Gastric Gland (Stomach)	Gastric juice	Pepsin	pH = 1–2 (acidic)	Protein	Peptides
Pancreatic Glands (pancreas)	Pancreatic juice	Lipase	pH = 8 (alkaline)	Lipids	Fatty acids + Glycerol
Liver (stored in gall bladder)	Bile	Bile salts (contains no enzymes)	pH = 8 (alkaline)	No substrate; it emulsifies lipids	Smaller droplets of lipids

Large intestine and adaptations to its functions

The large intestine is around 1.5 metres long. It consists of the **caecum**, **appendix**, **colon** and **rectum**. The remaining mixture of food that enters the large intestine is known as faeces.

Faeces consists of fibrous plant materials and large amounts of water from the digestive juices. Reabsorption of water from the faeces back into the blood is essential to prevent dehydration.

The large intestine is a natural habitat for some types of **mutualistic (symbiotic)** bacteria. One role of these bacteria is to produce some B vitamins and vitamin K for the body. Another type of bacteria digest some cellulose, releasing further nutrients for the body.

Adaptations of the large intestine to its functions

- Its length provides increased surface area for absorption.
- It is well-supplied with blood vessels for reabsorption of valuable materials.
- Goblet cells produce large amounts of mucus to ease the passage of faeces along the intestine.

The liver and bile

The liver is located in the upper abdomen, below the diaphragm.

- The liver is supplied with oxygenated blood through the **hepatic artery**.
- Digested food is brought, from the stomach and intestines, to the liver by the **hepatic portal vein**.
- The **hepatic vein** drains blood from the liver to the vena cava (see fig. 3.15, p. 113).

Functions of the liver

- It is the main storage site for carbohydrates. They are stored in the form of the polysaccharide **glycogen**. As the body needs energy, the liver converts glycogen to glucose and releases it into the blood.
- It breaks down excess protein (amino acids) to urea, in a process called **deamination**. The urea is then released into the blood. The kidney filters the urea from the blood and uses it to form part of urine.
- It produces bile.
- It breaks down and removes poisons from the blood.
- It produces body heat.
- It produces the protein fibrinogen for blood clotting.

Bile

Bile is a fluid produced by the liver and stored in the gall bladder. It is secreted, along the **bile duct**, into the duodenum to assist in digestion.

Functions of bile

- Bile salts emulsify lipids, speeding up their digestion.
- It is an alkaline fluid which neutralises acidic food from the stomach.
- It contains pigments produced from the breakdown of red blood cells (haemoglobin) in the liver.

Fibre

Fibre is made up of indigestible cellulose walls of plant material. A diet high in fibre is thought to prevent:

- bowel diseases like cancer
- obesity
- coronary heart disease.

2015 Q11 (a)/(b)/(c) HIGHER LEVEL

11. (a) (i) Humans are *heterotrophic* and *omnivorous.* Explain each of these terms.

(ii) What is meant by a balanced diet? **(9)**

(b) (i) Draw a large diagram of the human alimentary canal and its associated glands. On your diagram label all of the following:

1. Two associated glands. Name each gland labelled and put the letter *G* in brackets after each name to indicate it is a gland.

2. Two parts of the small intestine. Name each part labelled and put the letter *S* in brackets after each name to indicate it is part of the small intestine.

3. Two parts of the large intestine. Name each part labelled and put the letter *L* in brackets after each name to indicate it is part of the large intestine. **(27)**

(ii) Answer the following in relation to lipase.

1. What is lipase?

2. Give **one** part of the alimentary canal that secretes lipase.

3. What is the approximate pH at the site of the lipase action? **(27)**

(c) (i) 1. Write the dental formula for an adult human with a full set of teeth.

2. Give **one** difference between the dental formula referred to above and the tooth arrangement of the mammal in the photograph below.

3. What type of food do you think is mainly consumed by the mammal in the photograph? Explain your answer.

(ii) Give **two** functions of the large intestines.

(iii) Outline **two** beneficial functions of the bacteria that live in the digestive tract.

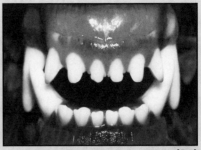

(24)

LEAVING CERT MARKING SCHEME

11. (a) (i) *Heterotrophic*: must consume food **or** eats other organisms **or** cannot make their food (3)

Omnivorous: eats both animal and plant (material) (3)

(ii) Correct amounts of each food type (for health) (3)

(b) (i) *Diagram*: continuous tube + stomach + intestines + a gland **(6, 3, 0)**

1. Liver / salivary glands / pancreas **(2[2, 1, 0])**

2. Duodenum / ileum **(2[2, 1, 0])**

3. Colon / caecum (or appendix) / rectum **(2[2, 1, 0])**

(ii) 1. Enzyme that digests lipids (**or** fats **or** oils) (3)

2. Stomach **or** duodenum [*accept* small intestine **or** ileum **or** salivary glands **or** pancreas] (3)

3. *Stomach*: (pH) < 7

Duodenum or small intestine or ileum: (pH) 7 – 9 (3)

(c) (i) 1. $I\dfrac{2}{2}\ C\dfrac{1}{1}\ PM\dfrac{2}{2}\ M\dfrac{3}{3}$ (3)

2. (Humans have) fewer incisors (or fewer canines) **or** Animal shown has more incisors (or more canines) (3)

3. *Type of food*: meat **or** flesh **or** other animals (3)

Explanation: long (**or** sharp **or** pointed **or** large **or** extra) canines (**or** incisors) (3)

(ii) Absorption of water / peristalsis / egestion / absorb vitamins 2(3)

(iii) Production of vitamins / compete with other micro-organisms / digestion / benefit immune system 2(3)

3.4 Breathing System and Excretion

Definitions
- Homeostasis
- Gaseous exchange
- Stomata
- Diffusion
- Lenticels

Outline
- Necessity of homeostasis
- Structure and diagram of respiratory system in humans
- Adaptations of the human respiratory system for gaseous exchange
- Cause, prevention and treatment of one breathing disorder
- Mechanism of breathing (inspiration and expiration)

- Effect of carbon dioxide levels on gaseous exchange in plants and animals

Homeostasis

Animal life is dependent on a constant internal environment. Cells function best in a specific, limited range of conditions. These conditions are both internal and external, in the surrounding fluids of the cells.

> **Homeostasis** is the regulation and maintenance of a constant internal environment in an organism.

Necessity of homeostasis

Enzymes, which control all metabolic reactions in organisms, are usually very sensitive to factors such as temperature and pH. The regulation of these factors is essential for optimal metabolism in the organism.

In humans, homeostasis is essential for:

- Regulation of blood sugar levels (see p. 149).
- The control of the concentrations of respiratory gases in the blood (see p. 138).
- Regulation of heartbeat rate (see p. 116).
- Control of the water content of the blood (see p. 142).
- Body temperature regulation (see p. 158).

Homeostasis in plants

One form of homeostasis in plants is the control of **gaseous exchange**. This occurs by the regulation of the size of the **stomata**. The **guard cells** controlling stomatal size are thought to be sensitive to CO_2 concentrations. This allows for the regulation of gaseous exchange to ensure there is sufficient CO_2 for photosynthesis and yet prevent the build-up of excess CO_2 when it is not required. (See fig. 2.17 on page 51.)

Lenticels are small pores on the stems of plants that also carry out gaseous exchange. They respond to conditions in a similar manner to stomata.

Breathing system in the human

Breathing (gaseous exchange) is the means by which oxygen is passed from the atmosphere into the blood, and by which carbon dioxide and water are passed from the blood into the atmosphere.

Respiratory system (Breathing system)

The respiratory system consists of:

- **The lungs**, which are highly vascular (contain enormous numbers of blood vessels) and contain many **bronchioles**, which end in microscopic air sacs called **alveoli**.
- The air passages are in the following sequence: mouth + nasal passages, pharynx, larynx, trachea, bronchi, bronchioles and alveoli.
- **Breathing muscles:**
  - The **intercostal muscles** join most of the ribs to one another so that a sheet of muscle covers the rib cage.
  - The **diaphragm muscles** form a seal under the lungs, separating them from the rest of the lower body organs (see fig. 3.25).

Gaseous exchange in humans

This is the movement of oxygen from the air into the blood and the movement of carbon dioxide from the blood into the air. It occurs in the alveoli of the lungs. Gaseous exchange occurs by **diffusion** (see fig. 3.26).

Adaptations of the respiratory system to gaseous exchange

- The nasal passages are lined with mucus and hairs which trap any dust particles entering with the air.
- The trachea and bronchi are lined with mucus and cilia to remove any remaining dust particles.
- The trachea and bronchi have rings of supporting cartilage which maintain an open air passage.
- Air is heated as it passes through the passages to the alveoli. This facilitates gaseous exchange by diffusion.

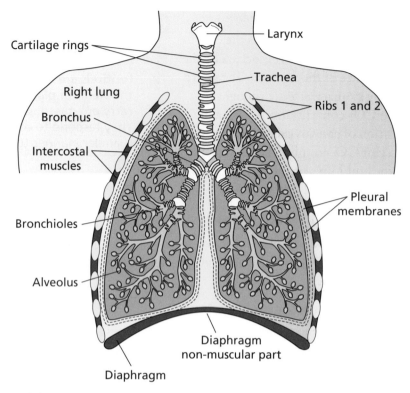

Figure 3.25 Respiratory system

Adaptations of the alveoli to facilitate gaseous exchange

- Alveoli have thin walls.
- Numerous alveoli create a very large surface area.
- Alveoli have a moist surface.
- Thin-walled capillaries surround the alveoli.

Mechanism of breathing

Breathing occurs in two stages.

1. **Inspiration:** The taking in of air from the atmosphere.
2. **Expiration:** The passing out of air to the atmosphere.

Inspiration is **active**, i.e. it requires the use of energy.

It occurs when:

- Intercostal muscles contract causing the rib cage to lift up and out.
- Diaphragm muscles contract, flattening the diaphragm.

Both of these actions increase the volume of the chest cavity, **reducing the pressure** of the air inside. Air then flows from the atmosphere into the lungs.

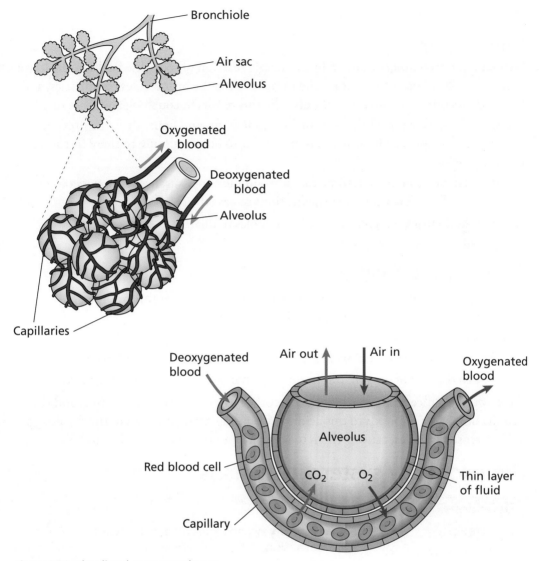

Figure 3.26 Alveoli and gaseous exchange

Expiration is **passive**, i.e. it does not require the use of energy (unless the body undergoes strenuous exercise).

It occurs when:

- The intercostal muscles relax, lowering the ribs.
- The diaphragm muscles relax, allowing the diaphragm to rise up.

Both actions cause the volume of the chest cavity to decrease, **increasing the pressure** of the air inside. Air then flows from the lungs into the atmosphere.

Breathing disorders

Asthma

Asthma is most commonly caused by an allergic reaction of specialised cells in the lower air passages. These mast cells release chemicals causing the bronchioles to constrict, and fluid and mucus to accumulate in the alveoli. This results in coughing and wheezing.

Causes: Allergens that cause asthma include pollen, fur and house dust. To prevent or reduce the incidence of asthma, it is important to limit exposure to these factors as much as possible.

Treatments: Treatment for asthma can be as simple as reassurance, as anxiety often worsens the effects. Two common medications to ease the symptoms are:

1. **Bronchodilators**, which cause the bronchioles to dilate.
2. **Steroids**, which reduce the inflammation.

 ## Control of breathing

Although we can consciously control breathing, it is usually controlled by an unconscious part of the brain, the **medulla oblongata**.

When we exercise:

- The amount of carbon dioxide in the blood increases, due to respiration.
- Due to the lack of oxygen, respiration becomes **anaerobic**, producing **lactic acid**.

These two substances cause the blood to become more acidic (lowers the pH) and the medulla oblongata responds to this acidity by sending nerve impulses to the diaphragm and intercostal muscles, causing them to contract and relax more quickly and deeply.

The excretory system in humans

Definitions	Outline
• Excretion • Reabsorption • Diffusion • Osmosis • Active transport	• Excretory organs and substances excreted from each (skin, lungs and kidneys) • Macro structure of kidney (cortex, medulla and renal pelvis) • Diagram of the urinary system (including blood supply) • Basic process of filtration and reabsorption in the kidneys • Pathway of urine from the kidney to urethra • Labelled diagram of nephron and blood supply • Detailed process of filtration and reabsorption along the nephron • Processes of reabsorption for glucose, amino acids, salts and water (diffusion, osmosis and active transport) • Reabsorption of water in the collecting duct and the role of ADH

Excretion is the removal of the waste products of metabolism from the body.

There are three main organs of excretion.

- The **lungs** excrete CO_2 and H_2O.
- The **kidneys** excrete urea, uric acid, excess water and salts.
- The **skin** excretes salts, water and uric acid.

Urinary system and the nephron

The urinary system consists of two kidneys and their blood vessels, two ureters, the bladder and the urethra (see fig. 3.27).

The kidneys have two functions.

1. Excretion
2. Osmoregulation

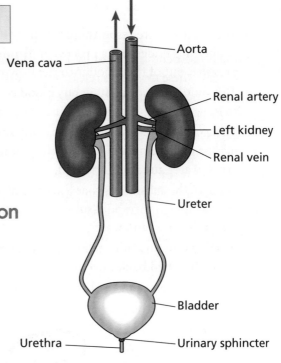

Figure 3.27 Urinary system

Excretion

The kidneys produce urine, which is excreted from the body. Urine consists of urea, excess water and excess salts. A vertical section (V.S.) through the kidney is shown in fig. 3.28.

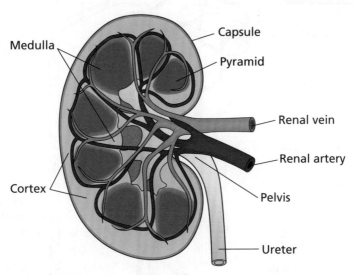

Figure 3.28 Vertical section of kidney (macrostructure)

Each kidney is made up of millions of filtration units called **nephrons.**

HL Filtration and reabsorption

- The nephrons are responsible for the formation of urine. The blood in the glomerulus undergoes a process of **ultrafiltration** which forces fluid, under pressure, out of the blood into the Bowman's capsule (see fig. 3.29).
- This fluid does not contain any blood cells or blood proteins, as they are too large to leave the glomerulus. The fluid is known as the **glomerular filtrate**.
- The glomerular filtrate contains many small molecules that were dissolved in the plasma of the blood. Wastes in the glomerular filtrate include excess salts and excess water, urea and uric acid.
- Some of the substances that leave the blood are very valuable to the body. These are called high threshold substances and include glucose, amino acids, vitamins, minerals (ions) and water.
- As the glomerular filtrate flows through the nephron, these **valuable substances are reabsorbed back** into the blood.
- Reabsorption occurs by **diffusion, osmosis** and **active transport**.

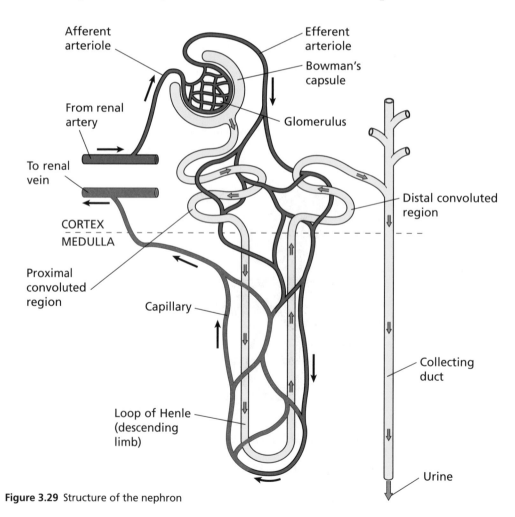

Figure 3.29 Structure of the nephron

Blood cells and blood proteins do not leave the blood during filtration. They are too large to pass into the glomerular filtrate.

Reabsorption is the process where high threshold substances are taken from the glomerular filtrate and returned to the blood. It can only occur by osmosis, diffusion and active transport.

Secretion is the process where substances are passed from the kidney cells into the glomerular filtrate, e.g. some ions (H^+) are secreted from the kidney cells into the glomerular filtrate.

Summary of substances reabsorbed

Substance	Region	Process
Glucose	Proximal convoluted region (PCR)	Active transport
Amino Acids	PCR	Active transport
Vitamins	PCR	Active transport
Salts	PCR	Active transport
Na^+ and Cl^-	Ascending limb of loop of Henle	Active transport
Na^+ and Cl^-	Distal convoluted region	Active transport
Water	PCR	Osmosis
	Loop of Henle	Osmosis
	Collecting duct	Osmosis

The nephron is adapted for filtration and reabsorption by:
- having a large surface area
- tubule wall being only one cell thick
- having porous walls.

Osmoregulation

Osmoregulation is the control of the salt/water balance in the body.

Osmoregulation is vital to keep the internal environment in the body constant.

- Too much water in the blood would lead to cells absorbing excess water by osmosis.
- Too little water or too much salt in the blood would lead to excess loss of water from the cells by osmosis.

Either condition would destroy the cells' ability to function.

 ## ADH

Diuresis is the production of excess watery urine. The antidiuretic hormone (ADH) prevents the production of large amounts of watery urine.

If there is too little water (or too much salt) in the blood:

- The **pituitary** gland produces more ADH.
- ADH causes the **collecting ducts** of the nephrons to become more permeable to water.
- More water can then be reabsorbed from the urine back into the blood before it leaves the kidneys.

2016 Q12 (a) (b) HIGHER LEVEL

12. (a) (i) Distinguish between the terms *excretion* and *egestion* by writing a sentence about each term.

    (ii) Suggest how excretion may occur in simple organisms such as *Amoeba*. **(9)**

  (b) (i) Name **two** excretory products, other than water, of mammals.

    (ii) For **each** product referred to in (i), give a location in the body in which it is produced.

    (iii) Describe the role of ADH (vasopressin) in human excretion.

    (iv) Suggest **two** structures in flowering plants which play a role in excretion. **(27)**

LEAVING CERT MARKING SCHEME

12. (a) (i) *Excretion:* Removal of metabolic waste **(3)**

        Egestion: Removal of undigested (or unabsorbed) material **(3)**

    (ii) *Simple excretion:* Diffusion **or** contractile vacuole **(3)**

  (b) (i) *Excretory products:* Carbon dioxide / urea / salt(s) **(2[3])**

    (ii) *Excretory product production locations:*

        First product + matching location **(3)**

        Second product + matching location **(3)**

(iii)   *ADH:* (Produced in response to) high salt levels or low water levels or dehydration / (acts on) collecting ducts or (acts on) distal convoluted tubules / more permeable / more water reabsorbed (into blood) / urine volume lowered (or urine more conc.)   **(3[3])**

(iv)   *Plant structures:* Stomata / lenticels / leaves   **(2[3])**

2015 Q6 HIGHER LEVEL   HL

6.   The diagram shows a vertical section through human skin.

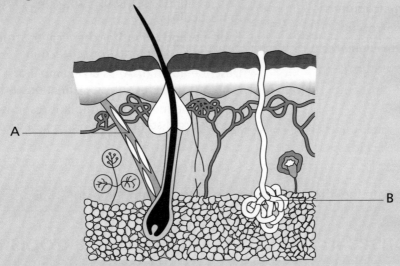

(a)   Place an X on the adipose tissue.

(b)   Name A and B.

(c)   Define each of the following words **and** explain how each process keeps the human body warm.

(i)   Piloerection.

(ii)   Vasoconstriction.

LEAVING CERT MARKING SCHEME

6.   8 + 7 + 5(1)

(a)   X correctly placed on adipose tissue

(b)   A = erector muscle

B = sweat gland

(c)   (i)   *Piloerection:* Hair stands up

Air is trapped **or** (air) insulates **or** reduces (or prevents) heat loss

(ii)   *Vasoconstriction:* Blood vessels (or arteries or arterioles) narrow

Reducing (or preventing) heat loss **or** less blood to skin

Responses in the flowering plant and tropisms

A **tropism** is the response of a plant to an external stimulus.

There are different types of tropisms.
- **Phototropism** is the response to light.
- **Geotropism** is the response to gravity.
- **Hydrotropism** is the response to water.
- **Thigmatropism** is the response to touch.
- **Chemotropism** is the response to chemicals.

Phototropism

Phototropism is the response of a plant to light.
- The **shoots** of plants are **positively** phototropic. If exposed to unilateral light, the shoot always grows towards it. This ensures the plant leaves have maximum light for photosynthesis.
- **Roots** are **negatively** phototropic. The root response is to grow away from unilateral light. This response causes the root to grow down into the soil. The response will provide anchorage and a source of minerals and water.

Geotropism

Geotropism is the response of a plant to gravity. **Roots** are **positively** geotropic, while shoots are **negatively** geotropic.

Growth regulators

> A **growth regulator** is a chemical produced in the growing tips (meristematic cells) of plants. The chemical is then transported from cell to cell by active transport to the site of response, where growth is modified.

Auxin (IAA) is one growth regulator that plays a significant role in phototropism. The process of phototropism is thought to occur as follows.

- If a plant is exposed to unilateral light, auxin is produced in the growing tips and is transported down the stem.
- Lateral movement of the auxin occurs from the illuminated side to the shaded side.
- The increased concentration of auxin causes cell elongation on the shaded side.
- Light on the illuminated side causes any auxin present to degenerate and become inactive. (See fig. 3.30.)

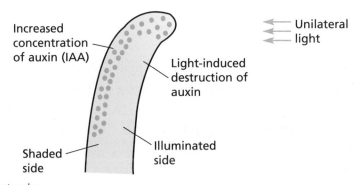

Figure 3.30 Phototropism

Note: Growth inhibitors seem to play a role in geotropism. Abscisic acid is an inhibitor that has been detected in shoots responding to gravity.

Uses of growth regulators in industry

Growth Regulator	Effects	Applications
Auxin (IAA)	(a) **In stems:** Promotes cell enlargement, cell division	(a) Speeds up primary and secondary growth in plants
	(b) **In roots:** Promotes root development in low concentrations	(b) Used as rooting powders for plant cuttings
Ethene	Stimulates the ripening of fruits	Prepare fruits for consumption after transportation

Adaptations of plants to adverse environmental conditions

Many plants have developed a number of features **to survive adverse conditions**.

- **Stinging chemicals** can deter grazing animals.
- **Heat-shock proteins** are produced by some plants in response to rising temperatures. These stabilise enzymes that could otherwise denature.
- **Poisons** in the leaves can protect against herbivorous insects.
- **Thorns** on the stems can protect softer, more vulnerable parts of the plant.

Mandatory activity

To investigate the effect of IAA growth regulator on plant tissue

Note: *The extra information in brackets below is not required when describing the procedure.*

Preparation of the IAA solutions (Serial dilutions)

1. Label eight sterile 15 ml bottles and eight Petri dishes with the following labels: 10^2 ppm, 10^1 ppm, 1 ppm, 10^{-1} ppm, 10^{-2} ppm, 10^{-3} ppm, 10^{-4} ppm and distilled water (*this acts as a control*).
2. Using a syringe, add 10 cm^3 of a prepared 10^2 ppm IAA solution to the first bottle.
3. Add 9 cm^3 of distilled water to each of the other seven bottles.
4. Using a graduated dropper, remove 1 cm^3 of the IAA solution and add it to the second bottle. Place the cap on the bottle and mix. (*This ensures the IAA is evenly distributed in the solution.*)
5. Using a new graduated dropper (*this prevents mixing of solutions*), remove 1 cm^3 of the IAA solution in the second bottle and add it to the third bottle. Place the cap on the bottle and mix.
6. Repeat this procedure of **serial dilutions** for the fourth, fifth, sixth and seventh bottles.
7. Finally, remove 1 cm^3 from the seventh bottle.
8. Place 9 cm^3 of distilled water in the last bottle (*the control*). Now all seven bottles have 9 cm^3 of the correct dilutions of IAA.

Setting up the petri dishes

1. Place a **circular acetate grid** inside the lid of the Petri dish labelled 10^2 ppm. (*The grid allows for easy measurement of growth.*)
2. Place five **radish seeds** along the central line of the grid (see fig. 3.31).
3. Cover the seeds with filter paper and pour some of the 10^2 ppm IAA solution onto it. (*This softens it.*)
4. Place cotton wool over the filter paper. (*To hold the radish seeds in place.*)

5. Pour the rest of the bottle over the cotton wool.
6. Place the base of the Petri dish onto the lid and seal the dish with some masking tape.
7. Repeat steps 1 to 6 for all the bottles and their Petri dishes.
8. Stand all the **dishes vertically** and leave in an incubator at 20 °C for two days. (*Vertical position ensures all growth is along the acetate grid.*)

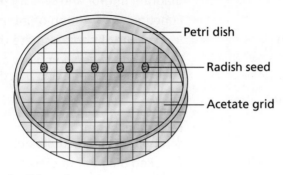

Figure 3.31 Positioning of radish seeds

Results and calculations

1. For each Petri dish, measure the length of all five shoots and all five roots produced from the seeds.
2. Calculate the average growth for shoots and then the roots.
3. To calculate the per cent stimulation or inhibition, use the following formula:

$$\frac{(\text{average length} - \text{average length of control})}{\text{average length of control}} \times 100$$

4. Draw a graph of the per cent stimulation/inhibition against the IAA concentration. (Place IAA concentration on the horizontal axis.)

Expected results

Generally IAA concentrations of 1 ppm stimulate shoot elongation and inhibit root growth. A concentration of 10^{-4} ppm stimulates root elongation.

Responses in humans

Definitions
- Central nervous system
- Peripheral nervous system
- Reflex action
- Sensory neuron
- Motor neuron
- Synapse
- Neurotransmitter
- Reflex action
- Reflex arc*

defined in the glossary

Outline
- Components of central and peripheral nervous system
- Neuron – structure, function and labelled diagram (motor and sensory neurons)
- Function and location of interneurons
- Movement of nerve impulse through a neuron
- Movement of nerve impulse across a synapse including activation and inactivation of neurotransmitters
- Structure and functions of the brain including cerebrum, hypothalamus, pituitary gland, cerebellum and medulla oblongata
- Labelled diagram of cross section of spinal cord including white matter, grey matter, central canal, meninges and dorsal and ventral roots of peripheral nerves
- Labelled diagram of reflex arc and mechanism of reflex action
- One disorder of the nervous system including possible cause, effect and treatment

There are two systems of sensitivity in animals.

1. Nervous system
2. Endocrine system

Nervous system

The nervous system consists of:

- **Central nervous system (CNS):** The brain and spinal cord.
- **Peripheral nervous system (PNS):** All the nerves attached to the central nervous system.

Central nervous system – brain and spinal cord

The brain consists of two hemispheres. The larger parts include a cerebrum, cerebellum and a medulla oblongata. The main parts of the brain are listed below (also see fig. 3.32a).

- **Cerebrum:** Carries out conscious thought processes and voluntary actions.
- **Cerebellum:** Controls balance and muscle co-ordination.
- **Medulla oblongata:** Controls breathing and heartbeat.

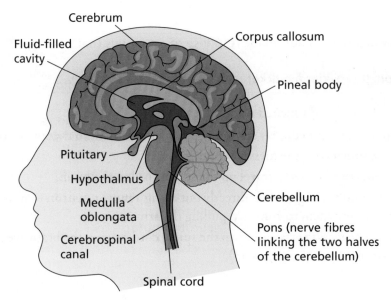

Figure 3.32a Human brain

- The **hypothalamus** is mainly concerned with homeostasis, i.e. the maintenance of a constant internal environment. It monitors levels of sugars and hormones in the blood.
- The **pituitary gland** controls the secretions of most endocrine glands in the body.

The **spinal cord** extends down through the vertebral column of the back. Pairs of peripheral nerves are attached to the spinal cord along its length (see fig. 3.32b). The spinal cord has two main areas.

- **White matter**, on the outside, which is made up of nerve fibres.
- **Grey matter**, on the inside, consists mainly of cell bodies.

> **key point**
>
> Nerve fibres carrying impulses away from the cell body are **axons**.
>
> Nerve fibres carrying impulses into the cell body are **dendrons**.

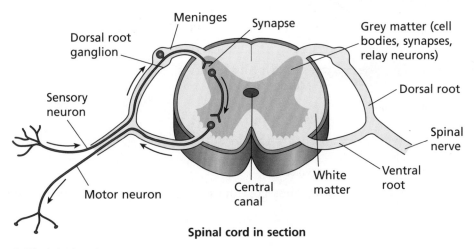

Spinal cord in section

Figure 3.32b Spinal cord

Reflex action (Arc)

> A **reflex action** is an automatic response to a stimulus that does not involve the brain.
>
> **Function:** It provides a quicker response to protect the body.

Example: If our hand touched an object that was too hot.

- A message is immediately sent along a **sensory neuron** to the spinal cord.
- At the spinal cord the message splits in two.
- One message begins to travel up the spinal cord to the brain.
- The second message travels directly out along a **motor neuron** to muscles in the arm, causing them to contract, pulling the arm away.
- When the message travelling up the spinal cord reaches the brain, we feel the sensation of pain (see fig. 3.33).

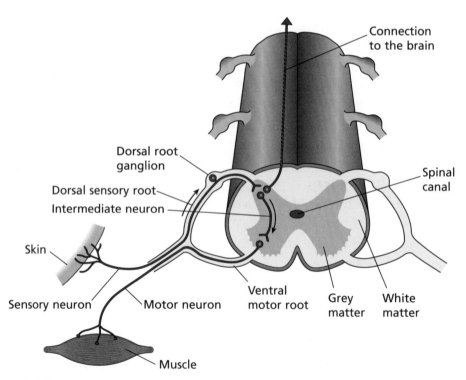

Figure 3.33 Reflex action

Neurons – nerve cells

There are two main types of nerve cells.

- **Sensory neurons** that bring messages from sense receptors in the body into the CNS (see fig. 3.34).

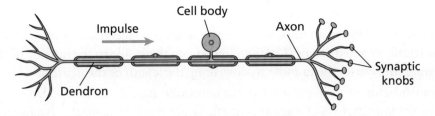

Figure 3.34 Sensory neuron

- **Motor neurons** that bring messages from the CNS out to effectors in the body (see fig. 3.35).

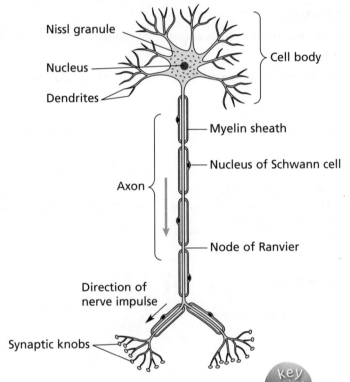

Figure 3.35 Motor neuron

Functions of neuron organelles

- **Myelin sheath:** Increases the speed of nerve impulse.
- **Schwann cell:** Secretes the myelin sheath which provides a faster rate of impulse transmission.
- **Axon:** Carries impulses away from the cell body.
- **Synaptic knob:** Secretes a chemical transmitter that passes an impulse from one neuron to the next.
- **Dendrite:** Initiates an impulse in a neuron, sending it towards the cell body.
- **Acetylcholine:** A chemical messenger that passes an impulse from the synaptic knob of one neuron to the dendrite of another across a synapse.

key point

A third type of neuron, known as an **interneuron**, is located in the spinal cord and acts as a link between a sensory neuron and a motor neuron in some reflex arcs.

Movement of nerve impulse

- The **transmission** of an impulse through a neuron is **electrical**. Movement of electrically charged atoms (Calcium ions) from the inside to the outside of the cell membranes causes the impulse to flow along the length of the neuron.
- **Transmission** of an impulse from one neuron to another is **chemical**. Neurotransmitter vesicles at the synaptic knobs release chemical messengers across the space between the neurons. This space is known as the **synapse**.
  - Neurotransmitters diffuse rapidly across the synapse to receptors on the next neuron.
  - Once the receptor is activated, the impulse begins, and the neurotransmitter becomes inactive.
  - This inactive form diffuses back across the synapse to the synaptic knob for reuse (see fig. 3.36).

Examples of neurotransmitters are **acetylcholine** (ACH) and **dopamine**.

Synapse

A **synapse** is a space between two neurons that are linked by chemical messengers. It allows for:

- impulses to be passed from one neuron to a number of neurons
- the protection of the response system from overstimulation, i.e. the supply of chemical messengers can be temporarily exhausted, ending the transmission of the impulse.

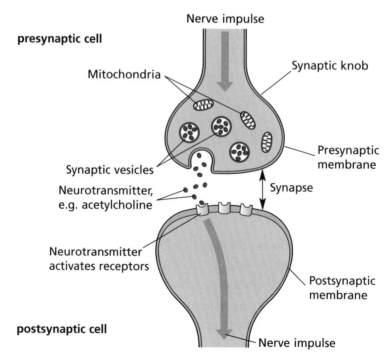

Figure 3.36 Synapse

Parkinson's disease

This is a **neurodegenerative** disease that affects voluntary control of muscles in the body.

Symptoms

It normally develops late in life and leads to progressive muscle stiffness, tremors and slowness of movement. In later stages of the disease, a general loss of motor coordination occurs.

Causes

Some parts of the brain (substantia nigra) do not produce sufficient amounts of the neurotransmitter dopamine. Dopamine is responsible for the stimulation of motor neurons. When dopamine production is depleted, the motor neurons are unable to control movement and coordination.

Treatment and prevention

There is no known cure for Parkinson's disease at present. Two possible treatments are being investigated.

- Dopamine cannot be given to a patient directly, as it cannot pass the blood–brain barrier. The drug Levodopa can, and it is converted to dopamine in the brain. Unfortunately, high concentrations of Levodopa can have harmful side effects.
- **Stem cell research** is exploring the possibility of replacing damaged cells with newly developed nerve cells.

Sense organs

Definitions	Outline
• Accommodation • Myopia • Hyperopia • Lens (convex and concave) • Binocular vision • Piloerection* • Vasoconstriction* *defined in the glossary	• Labelled diagrams for the eye, ear and skin • Corrective measures for an eye or ear defect

The three main **sense organs** are the **eye**, the **ear** and the **skin**.

The eye

The eye is sensitive to light. Images of reflected light from objects are focused on light-sensitive cells in the retina. Messages are then sent to the brain to create the sense of sight (see fig. 3.37).

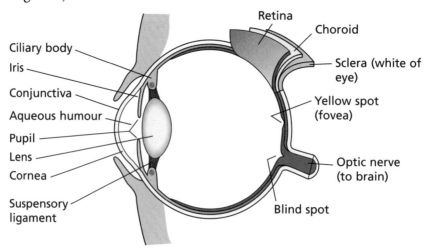

Figure 3.37 The eye

- **Lens:** Focuses light onto the retina.
- **Cornea:** Protects the front of the eye and allows light to enter.
- **Iris:** Controls the amount of light entering the eye. The muscles in the iris contract in bright light to reduce the size of the pupil.
- **Choroid:** Supplies blood to the eye.
- **Sclera:** Protects the eye.

The **fovea** is a shallow depression in the retina opposite the lens. It has large numbers of cone cells for colour vision.

- **Retina** is light-sensitive. It converts light into nerve impulses. There are two types of light-sensitive cells in the retina: rods and cones.

    1. **Rods** are not sensitive to colour and are used in poor light conditions.
    2. **Cones** are sensitive to colour and are used during the day.

Accommodation

Accommodation is the changing of the shape of the lens to focus light onto the retina.

The **ciliary muscle** (body) is a circular muscle around the lens.
When viewing distant objects:

- the ciliary body relaxes and stretches the lens.

When looking at near objects:

- the ciliary body contracts, allowing the lens to become thicker.

Eye defects

There are two main eye defects:

- Myopia (short sight)
- Hyperopia (long sight)

Myopia

Myopia is a condition where an individual can see close objects clearly, but distant objects are blurred. Myopia occurs when the lens focuses the image in front of the retina, resulting in a blurred image when the light strikes the retina.
Myopia can be corrected using a **concave** lens (see fig. 3.38).

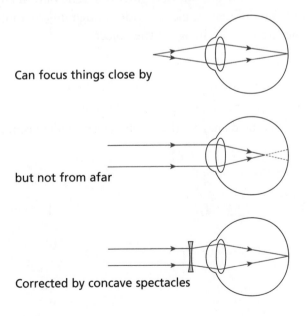

Can focus things close by

but not from afar

Corrected by concave spectacles

Figure 3.38 Myopia

Hyperopia

Hyperopia is a condition where an individual can see distant objects clearly, but close objects are blurred. Hyperopia occurs when the lens focuses the image behind the retina, resulting in a blurred image when the light strikes the retina.

Hyperopia can be corrected using a **convex** lens (see fig. 3.39).

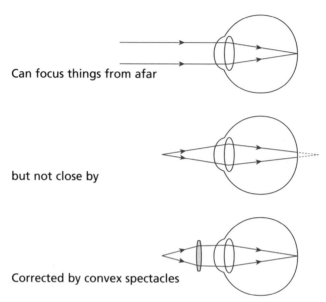

Can focus things from afar

but not close by

Corrected by convex spectacles

Figure 3.39 Hyperopia

Binocular vision

Humans have two eyes at the front of the head, providing **binocular vision**. Because the eyes are separated, each one provides a slightly different view of any object being observed. The views from different angles provide enough information for the brain to develop a three-dimensional (3D) image of the object.

Advantages of binocular vision

- The 3D image provides the sense of depth and distance.
- Two eyes provide a greater field of peripheral vision.
- Should one eye become damaged, the second eye provides vision.

The ear

The ear is concerned with both **hearing** and **balance**.

- The **cochlea** is responsible for hearing.
- The **semicircular canals** are responsible for balance (see fig. 3.40).

Hearing

- Sound is funnelled into the ear by the pinna.
- It causes the tympanum (eardrum) to vibrate.
- This movement is magnified by the three ossicles (bones), the malleus, incus and stapes.
- The stapes vibrates against a membrane called the fenestra ovalis.
- These movements in turn cause the fluids perilymph and endolymph to vibrate inside the cochlea.
- The vibrations stimulate sensory nerve cells, which send impulses to the brain along the auditory nerve.

Balance

Movements of the fluid endolymph in the **semicircular canals** of the inner ear are responsible for the sense of balance.

- Movement of the head in any particular direction will cause the movement of endolymph in one or more of the canals.
- **Sensory neurons** sensitive to this movement are located in the semicircular canals.
- Impulses are then passed to the brain by the auditory nerve.

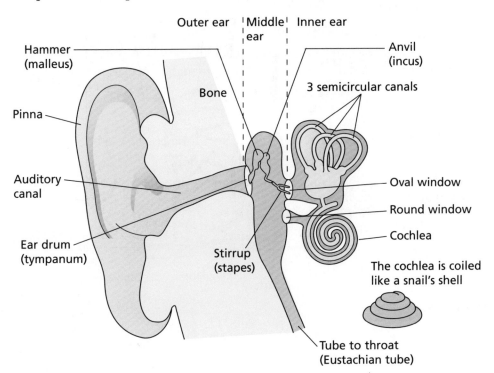

Figure 3.40 The ear

The skin

The skin acts as:

- an excretory organ
- a heat-regulating organ
- a sense organ (see fig. 3.41).

Heat regulation

When the body is too cold:

- **arterioles** near the skin surface contract, keeping blood away from the surface, reducing heat loss. The skin whitens.
- **erector muscles** contract, causing the hairs to stand up and trap a layer of air to act as an insulator.

If the body is too warm:

- **arterioles** widen to allow blood nearer the skin surface. This increases the rate of heat loss from the blood and the skin reddens.
- **sweat glands** release sweat. As the sweat evaporates, it carries heat energy away from the body.

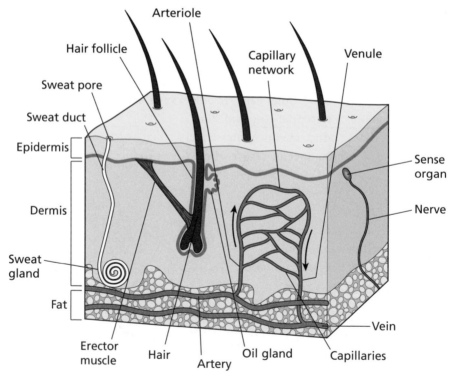

Figure 3.41 The skin

Endocrine system

The endocrine system is a system of co-ordination (sensitivity) in mammals. It consists of ductless glands that produce chemical messengers called hormones. Hormones are transported in the blood to a specific target where they produce a specific effect(s).

Endocrine and exocrine glands and hormones

Endocrine glands are ductless glands that release their cellular secretions (hormones) directly into blood capillaries.

Exocrine glands release their cellular secretions into a collecting duct before their release. Sweat and salivary glands are examples of exocrine glands.

> A **hormone** is a chemical messenger produced in small amounts by an endocrine gland. It is transported in the blood to a particular site, causing a specific effect. Hormones can be either protein or steroid in nature.

Summary of endocrine glands in the human

Gland	Location	Hormone	Function
Thyroid	Around larynx	Thyroxine	Controls metabolic rate of body cells
Parathyroids	Behind thyroid	Parathyroid Hormone	Controls calcium levels in the body
Adrenal	Above kidneys	Adrenaline	Prepares the body for high physical performance
Islets of Langerhans	In the pancreas	Insulin	Lowers blood glucose levels
Ovaries	Lower abdomen	(i) Oestrogen (ii) Progesterone	Builds up lining of uterus
Testes	Scrotum	Testosterone	Secondary sexual characteristics
Pituitary	Below forebrain	Growth Hormone (Somatotrophin)	Stimulates body growth

Insulin

Deficiency symptoms

A lack of insulin causes the blood glucose level to rise because the glucose cannot be converted to glycogen.

- If the amount of glucose in the blood rises above a certain level, the kidneys cannot reabsorb it all.
- The excess glucose is excreted in the urine.

This is known as **hyperglycaemia** and causes the disease diabetes mellitus. This is commonly known as insulin-dependent diabetes.

Symptoms: Lack of energy, persistent thirst and sometimes dizziness.

Treatment: This involves a carefully balanced diet related to physical activities to reduce insulin dependence. In many cases the individual injects monitored quantities of insulin directly into the blood.

Excess symptoms

Too much insulin in the blood causes a fall in blood glucose levels and can lead to **hypoglycaemia**.

Symptoms: Unconsciousness. In severe cases, coma and death can occur.

Hormone supplements

Hormone replacement therapy (HRT)

Menopause occurs in most women between the ages of 45 and 55 years. It results in the lowering of oestrogen and progesterone levels in the body. The effects of these hormonal changes are hot flushes, depression, anxiety and a significant decrease in bone density. This decrease in bone density can lead to a serious condition known as osteoporosis.

Hormone replacement therapy (HRT) can reduce the effects of menopause. It involves taking supplementary doses of oestrogen and progesterone. HRT is not suitable for all individuals. Recent research has linked HRT with incidences of breast cancer in some women.

Erythropoietin (EPO)

EPO is a naturally occurring hormone produced in the kidneys to regulate red blood cell formation in bone marrow. The illegal use of supplementary EPO is known to occur in total body endurance sports such as road cycling and distance running. Excess EPO increases red blood cell production to unnatural levels, increasing the oxygen-carrying capacity of the blood. Research has shown that performance can be improved by up to 15 per cent in endurance events. Excessive use of EPO thickens the blood, causing stresses in the circulatory system. Clotting can occur in smaller blood vessels. In extreme cases, cardiac arrest can occur.

Feedback mechanisms – negative feedback inhibition

All organisms that require stable internal body conditions (homeostatic organisms) use **negative feedback** in their control systems. The endocrine system has many examples of **negative feedback inhibition**.

- The female menstrual cycle begins when the pituitary gland secretes the hormone FSH.
- This stimulates a graafian follicle to develop in the ovary. As the graafian follicle matures, it produces the hormone oestrogen.
- Rising levels of oestrogen in the blood inhibit the pituitary gland from further production of FSH.
- This prevents the development of any more graafian follicles in the ovary (see fig. 3.42).

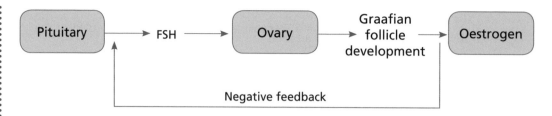

High levels of oestrogen inhibit the pituitary from producing more FSH

Figure 3.42 Negative feedback inhibition

Differences between endocrine and nervous systems

Nervous System	Endocrine System
1. Communication is by electrical-chemical impulses along nerve fibres	1. Communication is by chemical messengers in the blood
2. Impulses targeted to specific sites	2. Messages can be sent to many regions in the body
3. Causes muscles to contract or glands to secrete	3. Causes change in chemical reactions (metabolism)
4. Effects usually short-lived and reversible	4. Generally long-lasting effects

2016 Q13 (b)/(c) HIGHER LEVEL

13. (b) (i) Draw a large diagram to show the structure of the human ear, labelling each of the following parts:

pinna semi-circular canals stirrup

ear drum cochlea Eustachian tube

   (ii) 1. Briefly outline the function of the pinna.

   2. To which part of the body does the Eustachian tube link the ear?

   3. What is the role of the Eustachian tube?

   4. Name another part of the ear that has a function similar to that of the stirrup.

   5. The semi-circular canals play a role in balance. Suggest why there are three semi-circular canals in each ear. **(27)**

   (c) (i) Name the part of the eye that has a corresponding function to the cochlea of the ear. Explain your answer.

   (ii) Light passes through the pupil in the eye.

   1. Name the structure that determines the diameter of the pupil.

   2. Why is there a mechanism for changing the diameter of the pupil?

(iii) Certain parts of the eye are transparent and have curved surfaces.
1. Name **two** such parts.
2. How does the curvature contribute to the functioning of the eye?

(iv) The eyes of carnivores are located relatively close together at the front of the skull. In herbivores they tend to be located more to the sides of the skull. Referring clearly to either carnivores **or** herbivores, suggest a benefit of **either** arrangement

LEAVING CERT MARKING SCHEME

13. (b) (i) *Diagram:* with correctly located labelled parts   6(2)

pinna	**semi-circular canals**	**stirrup**
ear drum	**cochlea**	**Eustachian tube**

(ii) 1. *Function of pinna:* Collects sound   (3)
2. *Eustachian tube connected to:* Throat **or** pharynx   (3)
3. *Role of Eustachian tube:* To equalise pressure **or** to relieve (or prevent) pressure   (3)
4. *Other ossicle:* Hammer **or** anvil   (3)
5. *Why three semi-circular canals:* To control (balance) in three planes (or dimensions or axes)   (3)

(c) (i) Corresponding part of eye: *Retina **or** *fovea   (3)

Why: Both contain receptors (or both detect stimuli) **or** both generate impulses **or** both send impulses to the brain   (3)

(ii) 1. *Structure that determines pupil diameter:* *Iris   (3)
2. *Why pupil diameter changeable:* To control the amount of light entering the eye **or** to prevent too much light entering the eye **or** to let more light enter the eye   (3)

(iii) 1. *Transparent and curved:* Cornea   (3)
                        Lens   (3)
2. *How curvature helps eye:* To focus **or** to bend light **or** refract light   (3)

(iv) *Carnivores:* Better judgement of distance **or** better focus on prey

OR

Herbivores: Better detection of predators **or** wider field of vision (to detect predators)   (3)

2015 Q14 (b) HIGHER LEVEL

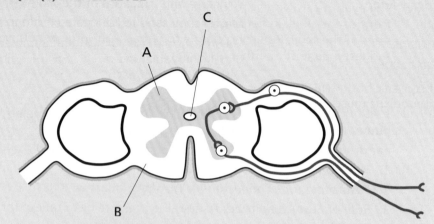

14. (b) (i) Name the parts labelled A, B and C in the diagram of the cross section of the spinal cord.

(ii) What is the main structural difference between A and B?

(iii) 1. What is the function of the meninges?

2. How many layers are present in the meninges?

(iv) Reflex actions are very important in animals.

1. What is a reflex action?

2. Outline the mechanism of a reflex action.

LEAVING CERT MARKING SCHEME

14. (b) (i) A = *grey matter (1)

B = *white matter (1)

C = *central canal **or** *cerebrospinal fluid (CSF) (1)

(ii) *A*: consists (mainly) of cell bodies **or** (mostly) no myelin (3)

B: consists (mainly) of axons **or** (mostly) myelin (3)

(iii) 1. Protection (of CNS) (3)

2. *Three (3)

(iv) 1. Automatic (or involuntary) response to a stimulus (3)

2. Stimulus at receptor / (causes) impulse along sensory neuron / (impulse) through interneuron / (impulse) through motor neuron / to effector (or muscle or gland) or effector reacts / (another impulse is sent) to the brain. **Any two 2(6)**

Musculoskeletal system

Definitions
- Endoskeleton
- Bone
- Cartilage
- Ossification
- Joint
- Antagonistic muscles

Outline
- Structure and functions of the skeleton
- Macroscopic labelled diagram of a long bone
- Classification of joints including immovable, slightly movable and freely movable joints with examples of each
- Labelled diagram of a synovial joint
- One musculoskeletal disorder including cause, prevention and treatment
- Role of antagonistic pairs of muscles with one example
- Location, structure and functions of:
  - Cartilage
  - Compact bone
  - Spongy bone
  - Red bone marrow
  - Yellow bone marrow
  - Ligaments
  - Tendons
  - Vertebral discs
- Role of osteoblasts in bone development (HL)

Human skeleton

The skeleton in vertebrates (animals with backbones) is an **endoskeleton**. It is a rigid framework of **bone** and **cartilage**. The endoskeleton is inside the body. Muscles involved in movement are outside the skeleton (see fig. 3.43).

Functions of the skeleton:
- **Support:** It provides shape and support for the soft body.
- **Protection:** It protects internal organs, e.g. the heart and lungs.
- **Movement:** It provides solid points of attachment for muscles to act on.

Structure of bone

Bone is made up of organic and inorganic matter.
- The **organic matter** consists of **living cells** and **protein** (collagen).
- The **inorganic matter** consists of the **minerals calcium carbonate** and **calcium phosphate**.

There are two main types of bone:

1. Compact bone
2. Spongy bone

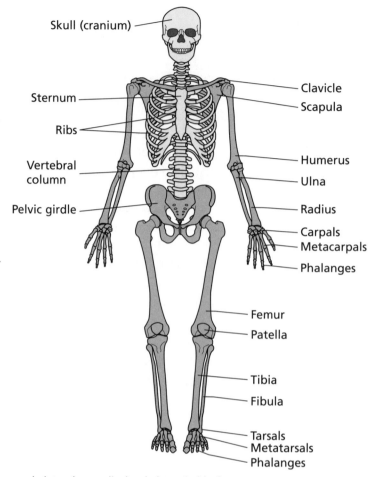

Figure 3.43 Human skeleton (appendicular skeleton in blue)

Compact bone

Compact bone is made up of Haversian systems packed together. Each Haversian system is made up of blood capillaries surrounded by concentric rings of tightly packed mineral bars called **lamellae**.

- Embedded in the lamellae are bone cells in small chambers called **lacunae**.
- Bone cells are responsible for laying down lamellae and producing new bone if a bone breaks.
- **Canaliculi** are blood capillaries that supply bone cells with nutrients.

Bone cells

There are three types of bone cells.

- **Osteocytes** are non-dividing inactive bone cells.
- **Osteoblasts** are actively dividing, laying down new lamellae.
- **Osteoclasts** reduce the size of bone by removing lamellae.

Bone growth

Bone is constantly changing during growth.

- Growth occurs at **growth plates**, located between the epiphysis and diaphysis of long bones.
- Growth plates produce **new cartilage** which is then ossified to bone.
- As adults, growth plates cease to function and no more growth occurs.

> **key point**
>
> Most compact bones are formed by **ossification**. In the foetus, the original skeleton of cartilage is filled with inorganic salts by the osteoblasts to form hard bone.

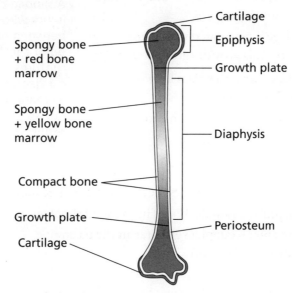

Figure 3.44 Macroscopic anatomy of a long bone

Spongy bone

Spongy bone consists of a network of hardened bars surrounded by **red bone marrow**.

- Red bone marrow is a soft tissue that is made up of cells that produce red blood cells and some white blood cells.

In long bones of the skeleton, compact bone surrounds a central core of **yellow bone marrow**.

- Yellow bone marrow stores fatty tissue and produces some types of white blood cells (see fig. 3.44).

Main bones in the body

Forelimb (Arm)

The bones in the arm are the humerus, radius and ulna, carpals (wrist), metacarpals (hand) and phalanges (fingers) (see fig. 3.43).

Hindlimb (Leg)

The bones in the leg are the femur, tibia and fibula, tarsals (ankle), metatarsals (foot), phalanges (toes).

Cartilage

Cartilage is a firm but flexible tissue, consisting of cells and some protein fibres. There are three types:

- **Hyaline cartilage** covers the surfaces of bones in movable joints. It contains some **collagen** (protein) fibres.

  Its functions are:

  (i) to reduce friction in movable joints

  (ii) to act as a shock absorber.

- **Elastic cartilage** is very flexible and provides shape in the outer ear.

- **Fibro-cartilage** is permeated with many collagen fibres. This provides great strength.

  Fibro-cartilage forms the **discs** between the vertebrae. Its functions are:

  (i) to reduce friction in movable joints

  (ii) to act as a shock absorber.

key point

A slipped disc refers to a back injury where a disc is pinched between two vertebrae. The outer cartilage of the disc ruptures and softer inner cartilage protrudes. This increases pressure on spinal nerves around this region and results in severe pain.

Joints

A joint is any point where two bones meet. There are three main types of joint:

- **Immovable joint**: Example: bones in the skull that have no movement.
- **Slightly movable**: Example: vertebrae in the backbone.
- **Synovial joint** (see fig. 3.45)

  Examples:

  o ball and socket joint (hip, shoulder)

  o hinge joint (knee, elbow, fingers)

  o gliding joint (wrist, ankle)

  o pivot joint (neck).

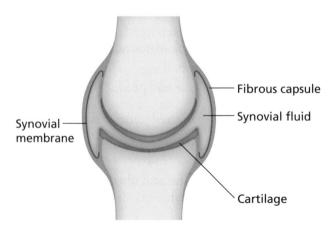

Figure 3.45 Synovial joint

Synovial joint

A **synovial joint** is freely movable. The parts of the two bones involved in the joint are covered with a layer of smooth cartilage. The synovial membrane produces synovial fluid, which lubricates the joint.

Ligaments

Ligaments are strong tissues with some flexibility. They are made of collagen.
Function: Ligaments hold bones together in a joint.

Tendons

Tendons are inelastic tissues made of collagen.
Function: Tendons attach muscles to bone to facilitate movement.

Antagonistic muscles

Voluntary muscles are attached to the skeleton and used for the movement of limbs. They work in pairs called **antagonistic pairs** that co-ordinate movement.
Example: the **triceps** and **biceps** of the upper arm.

- The biceps contracts and the triceps relaxes to raise the lower arm.
- To lower the arm, the triceps contracts and the biceps relaxes.

Musculoskeletal disorders

Arthritis

There are two common forms of arthritis:

1. Osteoarthritis
2. Rheumatoid arthritis

Osteoarthritis

Symptoms: A degenerative disease of the cartilage in movable joints. Much pain and stiffness can occur.
Causes: Obesity, low bone density and a genetic influence are all linked to the disease.
Treatment/prevention: Consistent light exercise of the affected joints can delay the onset of the symptoms. Treatments to alleviate the symptoms include weight loss and the use of painkillers and anti-inflammatory drugs.

Rheumatoid arthritis

Symptoms: A chronic inflammation of affected joints. Many joints are often affected at the same time.
Cause: It is caused when the immune system begins to attack normal tissues at the joints.
Treatment: This includes the use of anti-inflammatory drugs, exercise and in severe cases the replacement of joints.

Defence and the immune system

Definitions
- Immunity
- Natural immunity
- Induced immunity
- Antigen
- Lymphocyte
- Antibody
- Vaccine
- Immunisation
- Vaccination

Outline
- The first and second lines of defence including the roles of the
  - Skin
  - Breathing system
  - Reproductive system
  - Phagocytic white blood cells
- The specific defence system of induced immunity including
  - Antigen antibody response
  - Role of B and T Lymphocytes
  - Role of Helper, Killer, Suppressor and Memory T cells

Immunity is the ability of the body to resist the entry of pathogens, or the effects of their toxins.

Natural immunity

Natural immunity prevents the entry of pathogens into the body. It consists of two main lines of defence.

First line of defence

The **first line** of defence consists of:

- **The skin:** The skin is impregnated with keratin, which is an impermeable barrier. Sweat from sweat glands and a natural flora of bacteria inhibit the establishment of pathogens on the surface.
- **The respiratory system:** The nasal passages are lined with hairs to filter incoming air. The trachea and bronchi are lined with a sticky mucus and cilia to trap any unwanted particles in the air.
- **The digestive system:** The hydrochloric acid in the stomach can destroy pathogens taken in with food.
- **Mutualistic** (symbiotic) bacteria in the vagina secrete lactic acid which prevents the entry of pathogens.

Second line of defence

The second line of defence is the response of the body once the first line fails and pathogens have a point of entry into the body.

The second line of defence consists of:

- **Blood clotting:** This is a rapid response that seals a wound.
- **Phagocytic white blood cells:** These accumulate at the damaged site and attack any foreign objects.

Induced (acquired) immunity

If a pathogen evades the natural immunity of the body, the use of **induced** or **acquired immunity** is then necessary. A few important terms are defined below.

> Any foreign object (usually a pathogenic bacteria) in the body which causes the production of antibodies to destroy it is known as an **antigen**.
>
> A **lymphocyte** is a white blood cell stored in the lymphatic system that produces antibodies to destroy antigens.
>
> An **antibody** is a specific protein produced by lymphocytes in response to the presence of an antigen.
>
> A **vaccine** is a diluted or dead non-disease-causing dose of a pathogen. It stimulates antibody production. Vaccination activates immune response before infection occurs.
>
> **Immunisation** is the production of immunity by artificial means. It can occur by the administration of vaccines or antibodies.

There are two forms of induced immunity:

- active induced immunity
- passive induced immunity

Active induced immunity is where antibody production is stimulated by exposure to a particular antigen. There are two forms.

- Antibody production stimulated by exposure to a particular pathogen by natural means.
- Antibody production stimulated by the administration of a **vaccine**.

Passive induced immunity is where antibodies are supplied from an external source to fight disease. There are two examples.

- Antibodies injected into the body immediately after injury, e.g. anti-tetanus injection. **Note:** This is a very rapid form of immunity as there is no time delay in manufacturing antibodies.
- **Maternal antibodies** diffusing across the placenta to the foetus. Similarly, antibodies in breast milk provide immunity for the offspring.

key point

- Active immunity is long-lasting as the body can rapidly reproduce antibodies should exposure occur again.
- Passive immunity is short-lived as the antibodies are broken down by the body of the recipient.

(HL) Role of lymphocytes in immunity

There are two main types of lymphocytes in the body. These are known as B and T cell types.

B Lymphocytes

- B lymphocytes are produced in the **bone marrow** and migrate to the **lymph nodes**.
- When exposed to an antigen, the B cells replicate. Most of the cells produced provide large quantities of antibodies to destroy the antigen.
- Some of the cells produced remain in the lymph nodes as **memory cells**. They provide a very rapid response if a second exposure occurs to the antigen.

T Lymphocytes

- T lymphocytes are produced in the **thymus** gland and then migrate to the lymph nodes.
- There are four main types, each having different roles in the immune response.
    1. **Helper T cells** divide when exposed to an antigen. Some of the cells form Memory T cells, while others activate the different types of T cells, enhancing their effectiveness.
    2. **Killer T cells** attack large pathogens such as unicellular **parasites**. They can also destroy cancer cells or cells containing viruses. Killer T cells act by puncturing the cell membranes of pathogens.
    3. **Supressor T cells** regulate the immune system. They can suppress immune responses when appropriate.
    4. **Memory T cells** remain in the lymph nodes to provide a very rapid response if a second exposure to the antigen occurs.

Viruses – viral diseases and treatment

Viruses consist of a **protein coat** surrounding a **nucleic acid**, either DNA or RNA (see fig. 3.46).

With reference to the general characteristics of living things, scientists have difficulty classifying viruses as living organisms because:

- Viruses are non-cellular.
- They have no organelles and do not have a metabolism that exists in plant and animal cells and in bacteria.
- Viruses are described as **obligate parasites** since they can only reproduce inside a host cell by using its metabolism.
- Only one type of nucleic acid (DNA or RNA) can exist in any one virus.

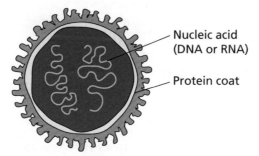

Nucleic acid
(DNA or RNA)

Protein coat

Figure 3.46 A virus

Harmful effects of viruses

Swine flu

Swine flu (H1N1) is an example of a disease caused by a virus. It affects the respiratory system, producing flu-like symptoms. The virus originated in pigs but evolved to infect humans. A mutation of this virus resulted in a strain that can be passed from human to human.

AIDS

AIDS is a disease caused by the HIV virus. HIV disables T cells, which are an essential part of the human defence system. The weakening of the immune system leaves the victim vulnerable to other life-threatening diseases.

Treatment of viral disease

Not having a metabolism similar to bacteria, viruses are immune to the effects of antibiotics.

Two methods of fighting viral disease are:

- Vaccines
- Anti-viral drugs

Vaccines

Vaccines can be very effective but must be administered before infection. For any new virus discovered, it can take up to six months to develop sufficient quantities of an effective vaccine.

Anti-viral drugs

Anti-viral drugs can be prescribed after infection. They help reduce the severity of the symptoms and reduce the spread of the virus to new hosts.

key point

The rapid rate of **viral mutation** quickly renders both vaccines and anti-viral drugs obsolete.

Benefits of viruses

- **Genetic engineering** procedures use viruses as vectors to insert desirable genes from one organism into the host cells of a different organism.
- **Bacteriophages** are viruses that have the ability to attack bacteria. Investigations are ongoing as to their possible use to destroy pathogenic bacteria.

HL

2012 Q3 (a)/(b) HIGHER LEVEL

3. (a) The diagram shows the macroscopic structure of part of a long bone.
   (i) Name a long bone in the human body.
   (ii) Name parts X, Y and Z in the diagram.
   (iii) State a function of X.
   (iv) State a function of Y.
   (b) (i) Show clearly on the diagram where you would expect to find cartilage.
   (ii) State **one** role of **this** cartilage.

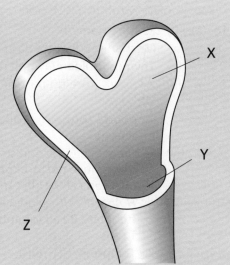

LEAVING CERT MARKING SCHEME

3. 2(7) + 4(1)
   (a) (i) E.g. femur, tibia, fibula, humerus, radius, ulna
   (ii) X = spongy bone **or** marrow; Y = medullary cavity **or** marrow; Z = compact bone
   (iii) X: Strength (or rigidity) **or** lowers density **or** makes blood cells (or named) **or** makes marrow
   (iv) Y: Makes (yellow) marrow **or** stores fat **or** makes blood cells (or named)
   (b) (i) Indication of cartilage on diagram
   (ii) Prevents bond damage **or** friction free movement **or** shock absorption

HL

2015 Q14 (a) HIGHER LEVEL

14. Answer any **two** of (a), (b), (c).   (30, 30)
   (a) (i) Outline how any **one** named feature of the human general defence system works.
   (ii) Name **two** organs in the human body that are specific to the immune system.
   (iii) Distinguish clearly between an antigen and an antibody.
   (iv) T cells are a type of lymphocyte, with different sub-types having different roles in our immune system.
      1. Describe the specific roles of both killer T cells **and** helper T cells in an immune response.
      2. Name the T cells that stop the immune response.

LEAVING CERT MARKING SCHEME

14. (a) (i) Feature named (3)

Mechanism described (3)

(ii) Thymus / spleen / lymph nodes / tonsils (2[3])

(iii) *Antigen*: (foreign particle that) causes an antibody response

OR

Antibody: (protein) produced in response to an antigen (or to infection) (3)

(iv) 1. *Killer T cells*: recognise infected cell (or cancer or antigen) **or** produce perforin **or** perforates (cell) membrane **or** kill the infected cell **or** kill cancer cell (6)

Helper T cells: produce interferon **or** recognise antigens **or** stimulate B-cell (or antibody production) **or** activate Killer T cells (6)

2. *Suppressor (T cells) (3)

Sexual reproduction in the flowering plant

Definitions
- Pollination
- Fertilisation
- Double fertilisation
- Fruit
- Germination
- Dormancy
- Vegetative propagation

Outline
- Structure and function of the flower (include labelled diagram)
- Structure of pollen grain and embryo sac (include labelled diagrams)
- Types of pollination (self and cross)
- Differences between wind and insect (animal) pollinated flowers
- Process of double fertilisation
- Seed structure (including testa, plumule, radicle, embryo and cotyledon(s))
- Labelled diagrams of endospermic and non-endospermic seeds
- Fruit formation and seed dispersal (including wind, water, animal and self dispersal)
- Factors necessary for germination
- Role of digestion and respiration in germination
- Dormancy and its advantages
- Labelled diagrams of examples of vegetative propagation in the stem, root, leaf and bud
- Four methods used for artificial propagation
- Process of mature pollen grain development from diploid mother cell (microspore)
- Process of mature embryo sac development from diploid mother cell (megaspore)

Practical Activities
- Investigate the effect of water, oxygen and temperature on germination
- Use of starch agar or skimmed milk plates to show digestive activity during germination

The flower

The flower is the sexual reproductive organ of the flowering plant (see fig. 3.47).

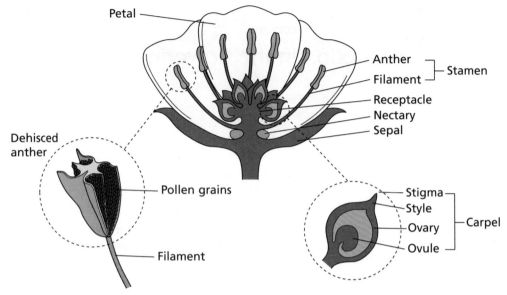

Figure 3.47 The flower

- The **sepals** are green and protect the developing flower bud.
- The **petals** are brightly coloured and can produce scent and nectar.
- The **stamens** produce the male pollen.
- The **carpels** produce the female embryo sac.

Pollen development

Pollen is produced in the anther of the stamen. The anther contains four pollen sacs.
The inner layer of each sac is called the tapetum and it nourishes the developing pollen.
Two haploid male gametes develop inside the pollen.

 ### Stages of pollen development

- Diploid (2n) microspore mother cells in the pollen sac divide by **meiosis** to form four haploid cells.
- Each haploid cell forms a pollen grain.
- The nucleus of the pollen grain divides once by **mitosis** to form a **tube nucleus (n)** and a **generative nucleus (n)** (see fig. 3.48).

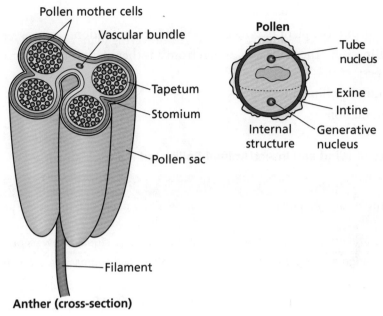

Figure 3.48 Pollen formation

Embryo sac development

The ovary of the carpel contains one or more **ovules**. A haploid egg cell and two haploid polar nuclei form in the ovule.

Stages of embryo sac development

- Inside each ovule a single diploid megaspore mother cell (2n) divides by meiosis to produce four haploid cells.
- Three degenerate and the nucleus of the one remaining divides by mitosis three times.
- The cell with its nuclei is known as the **embryo sac**.

Sexual reproduction

Sexual reproduction occurs in four stages:

1. Pollination
2. Fertilisation
3. Seed dispersal
4. Germination

1. Pollination

Pollination is the transfer of mature pollen from the stamen to the stigma of the carpel.

There are two main types of pollination:

1. **Self-pollination:** The plant uses its own pollen for fertilisation.
2. **Cross-pollination:** The plant uses pollen from another plant for fertilisation. There are two types:
   - Insect/animal pollination
   - Wind pollination

Characteristics of Wind and Insect/Animal-Pollinated Plants

Wind-Pollinated	Insect/Animal-Pollinated
1. Large quantities of light pollen produced	1. Small numbers of large, sticky pollen produced
2. No perfume and little colour in flower	2. Coloured, perfumed flowers produced
3. Anthers and stigmas hang outside the flower	3. Anthers and stigmas are protected inside the flower
4. No nectar produced	4. Nectar produced

2. Fertilisation

Fertilisation in the flowering plant

- The pollen grain germinates and the generative nucleus divides by mitosis to produce two male gamete nuclei (n).
- The tube nucleus grows down through the style and moves towards the micropyle by **chemotropism.**
- At the micropyle, the tube nucleus disintegrates and the two male gamete nuclei enter the embryo sac.
- Fertilisation in the flowering plant is known as **double fertilisation** because
  - Fusion of first male gamete nucleus with female egg produces the **zygote (2n).**
  - Fusion of second male gamete nucleus with the two polar nuclei forms a triploid (**3n**) **endosperm nucleus** (see fig. 3.49).

Fertilisation is the fusion of two haploid gametes to form a diploid zygote.

- The zygote develops to form the embryo (radicle, plumule and cotyledons).
- The endosperm nucleus develops to form an endosperm food store.

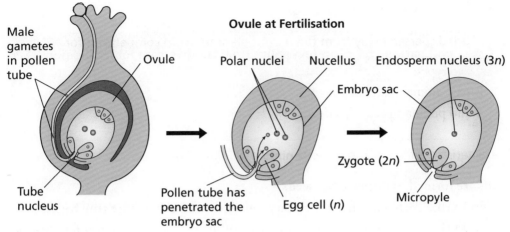

Figure 3.49 Fertilisation

Seed

The **seed** is formed from the **ovule** after fertilisation. The seed is a form which allows the plant to:

- survive the unfavourable season for young seedling growth
- ensure dispersal of offspring.

Two types of seed can be produced, depending on the location of stored food for the embryo:

1. **Non-endospermic seeds** (e.g. pea or bean) store food reserves in the cotyledon(s).
2. **Endospermic seeds** (e.g. corn or barley) store their food in the endosperm (see fig. 3.50).

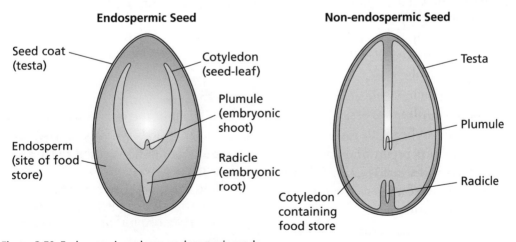

Figure 3.50 Endospermic and non-endospermic seeds

3. Fruits and seed dispersal

Seeds are dispersed away from the parent plant to avoid **competition** for
- light
- minerals
- water
- space

Fruits
Fruits are formed to disperse the seeds.
- Fruits that are formed from the ovary wall of the carpel alone are **true fruits**.
- Fruits that are formed from any other part of the flower are known as **false fruits**.

Methods of seed dispersal
There are four methods of seed dispersal:
- **Wind:** The seeds of the sycamore tree have **winged fruits** which make the seed spin on release. This slows the rate of fall and carries the seed away from the parent plant.
- **Animal:** The blackberry bush produces seeds with **succulent fruits**. Animals consume the seeds, depositing them undigested much later. The seeds are dispersed with the natural fertilizer of the animal faeces.
- **Water:** Water lily plants produce seeds with a **spongy, buoyant fruit**. This allows the water to carry the seeds away from the parent plant.
- **Self:** Pea plants produce their seeds inside **pods**. Tension increases as the pods dry out. Eventually the pod bursts, flicking the seeds away from the parent plant.

4. Germination

Germination is the beginning of the process of development of a seed to an adult plant.

Germination requires the presence of three factors:
1. **Water**
2. **Oxygen**
3. **Temperature**

- Germination begins when the seed absorbs water into its cells. This provides the medium for the seed enzymes to function.
- The enzymes **digest** the food stores (in the cotyledons or the endosperm), breaking them down to single units so they can be **translocated** to the growing embryo.

key point

- Much of the glucose produced during digestion is used for the process of respiration.
- Initially anaerobic respiration occurs, but as energy demands increase, respiration becomes aerobic.
- The energy released is used to fuel the processes of germination.

○ Starch is converted to glucose.

○ Protein is converted to amino acids.

○ Lipids are converted to fatty acids and then glucose.

Stages of seedling growth

- The **radicle** is first to emerge from the seed. It grows downwards into the soil, developing a root system and root hairs. The seedling now has anchorage and a source of water and minerals.
- The **plumule** then emerges, pushing above the soil. The plumule develops to form the stem and leaves.
- Once photosynthesis can occur, the seedling then manufactures its own food.

Mandatory activity

To investigate the effect of water, oxygen and temperature on germination

1. Soak 20 dried pea seeds in water for 24 hours.
2. Place five soaked seeds on moist cotton wool in test tube A and leave in an incubator at 25 °C.
3. Place five soaked seeds on moist cotton wool in test tube B and leave in a fridge at 4 °C.
4. Place five soaked seeds on moist cotton wool in test tube C with alkaline pyrogallol (to remove O_2). Seal with a stopper. Leave in an incubator at 20 °C.
5. Place five dry pea seeds on dry cotton wool in test tube D and leave in the incubator at 20 °C (see fig. 3.51).

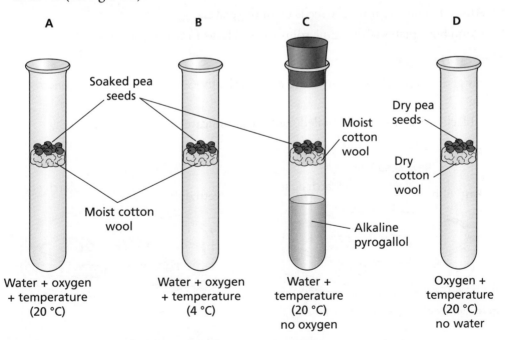

Figure 3.51 To investigate the effect of water, oxygen and temperature on germination

Expected results

The seeds in A germinate normally. The seeds in B, C and D do not germinate.

Mandatory activity

To show digestive activity during germination using starch agar or skimmed milk plates

Note: *The extra information in brackets below is not required when describing the procedure.*

1. Swab the laboratory bench with disinfectant (*reduces the possibility of contamination*).
2. Label one starch agar place 'test' and the other 'control'.
3. Kill two broad bean seeds by boiling in water for ten minutes.
4. Remove the testa and separate the cotyledons.
5. Soak the cotyledons in disinfectant for ten minutes (*this kills any surface micro-organisms*).
6. Rinse the seeds in sterilised water.
7. Flame a forceps in a Bunsen burner (*to sterilise it*) and allow it to cool.
8. Using the forceps, transfer the seed halves, face down, onto the surface of the starch agar on the **'control'** Petri dish.
9. Reflame the forceps and leave on the bench.
10. Repeat steps 4 to 8 using two **'live'** seeds, placing them in the dish labelled **'test'**.
11. Incubate both plates upright at 20 °C for two days.
12. After 48 hours, remove the seeds from the plates.
13. Flood both plates with iodine solution and leave for three minutes.

Expected results

Yellow areas on starch agar under and around the live seeds indicate the absence of starch.

Blue/black areas, only, in the boiled seeds' dish indicate the presence of starch.

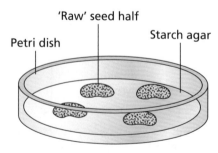 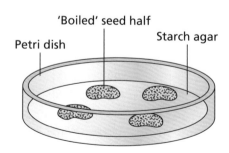

'Raw' seed half   Starch agar   'Boiled' seed half   Starch agar

Petri dish   Petri dish

Figure 3.52 'Test' and 'control' Petri dishes

Note: After the experiment is finished:

- Sterilise all materials used in a pressure cooker.
- Swab down the bench with disinfectant.

Dormancy

Dormancy is a condition where seeds do not germinate even though the factors of oxygen, temperature and water are present.

Dormancy ensures that a seed germinates at a time when climatic conditions are optimal.

Examples of dormancy

- Apple seeds do not germinate until after a long period of cold.
  - This ensures the seeds only germinate during the suitable conditions of spring, after winter. Earlier germination would expose the vulnerable seedlings to hazardous winter temperatures.
- Certain cactus plants in deserts produce seeds with **inhibitors** in their seed coats. The seeds will only germinate when there is enough water to wash the inhibitor out of the seed.
  - This helps ensure that germination will only occur in conditions of heavy, prolonged rainfall. Sufficient water is essential for the seedlings to establish themselves before drought conditions return.

Vegetative propagation

This is **asexual reproduction** in flowering plants. It does not involve the production of gametes or seeds and the offspring are **genetically identical** to the parent.

Different organs can be used for vegetative propagation, such as:

- **Stem:** The potato plant produces a modified underground stem tuber.
- **Root:** Dahlia is a modified root tuber.
- **Bud:** The onion is a modified bud.

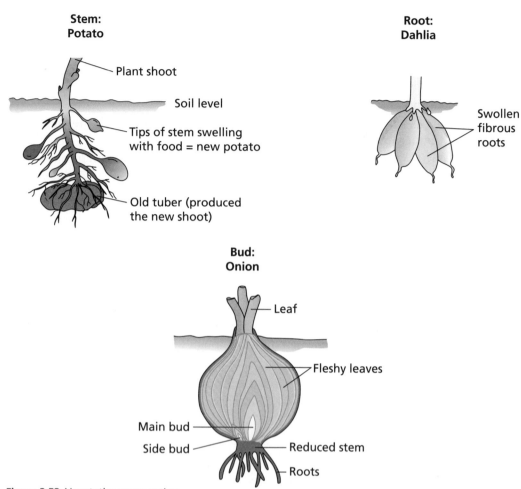

Stem:
Potato

Plant shoot

Soil level

Tips of stem swelling
with food = new potato

Old tuber (produced
the new shoot)

Root:
Dahlia

Swollen
fibrous
roots

Bud:
Onion

Leaf

Fleshy leaves

Main bud

Side bud

Reduced stem

Roots

Figure 3.53 Vegetative propagation

Comparison of vegetative propagation and sexual reproduction

Sexual Reproduction	Vegetative Propagation
1. There is genetic variation in the offspring. *This provides a greater chance of individuals surviving in adverse conditions*	1. All offspring are genetically identical. *A disease that affects one will affect all*
2. Seeds will be dispersed to avoid competition	2. Offspring grow very close to parents, increasing competition
3. Seeds may remain dormant in adverse conditions	3. Plants may survive adverse conditions by their modified roots, stem or leaves
4. Plants may take years to grow to maturity	4. Plants develop very rapidly
5. Many seeds are wasted	5. No wastage involving lost seeds
6. Offspring can never be genetically identical to the parent	6. Plants of a particular variety can be maintained

Artificial propagation

Horticulturists use methods of vegetative propagation that do not occur in nature.

(a) **Budding:** A vegetative bud (scion) is cut away from a plant. The bark of the new plant (stock) is cut to expose the cambium tissue and the vegetative bud is inserted. New xylem and phloem tissues connect the two parts.

(b) **Grafting:** An entire branch or stem (scion) is cut from one plant and attached to a newly cut stem of equal diameter of a second plant (stock). It is important that the cambia of both parts are in contact. New xylem and phloem then develop, linking both parts.

(c) **Cuttings:** A healthy branch is cut from a parent plant at a point between two nodes. The cut section is dipped in rooting powders and planted in very moist fresh soil. New roots develop from the base of the cutting.

(d) **Micropropagation:** This is also known as tissue culture propagation. Very small pieces of tissue (explants) are cut from the parent plant and are cultured in a sterile nutrient medium in a controlled environment. Growth regulators are then used to stimulate the production of roots and leaves in each sample.

2014 Q14 (a) HIGHER LEVEL   HL

14. Answer any **two** of (a), (b), (c).   (30, 30)

   (a) (i) Name:
        1. the site of production of a pollen grain **and**
        2. the structure on which it must land to complete pollination.

    (ii) Name **two** methods of cross pollination.

    (iii) Many species of plant have mechanisms that prevent self-pollination. Suggest how such plants could benefit from this.

    (iv) Describe in detail the events that follow the arrival of a pollen grain at the destination referred to in (i), up to and including fertilistation.

    (v) Which part of a flower usually develops into a fruit?

LEAVING CERT MARKING SCHEME

14. (a) (i) Anther [*accept* stamen]   **(3)**
         *Stigma   **(3)**
    (ii) Wind / animal (or example) / water   **(2[3])**
    (iii) Greater variation **or** explained **or** prevents inbreeding **or** explained   **(3)**

(iv) Pollen (grain) germinates **or** pollen tube produced / grows through style / generative nucleus divides by mitosis / to form 2 (male) gametes / entry into embryo sac / one (gamete) fertilises the egg (cell) / one fertilises the polar nuclei   **(4[3])**

(v) *Ovary

2012 Q14 (a) HIGHER LEVEL

14. Answer any **two** of (a), (b), (c).   **(30, 30)**

(a) (i) Give a brief account of the role of **each** of the following in flowering plant reproduction.

   1. Petal.

   2. Anther.

   3. Stigma.

(ii) Name **one** structure through which the pollen tube grows in order to reach the embryo sac.

(iii) Within the pollen tube the generative nucleus divides to form two male gametes.

   1. What type of division takes place?

   2. With what does **each** male gamete fuse in the embryo sac?

   3. Name the product of **each** fusion.

(iv) As the seed forms following fertilisation, a food store develops in one of two structures. Name any **one** of these structures.

LEAVING CERT MARKING SCHEME

14. (a) (i) 1. Attracts insects (or other pollinators)   **(3)**

   2. (Site of) pollen manufacture **or** (site of) pollen release   **(3)**

   3. Pollen lands on it **or** pollen sticks to it **or** pollen germination

(ii) Stigma **or** style **or** ovary **or** micropyle   **(3)**

(iii) 1. *mitosis   **(3)**

   2. egg [*allow ovum or female gamete*]   **(3)**

   polar nuclei   **(3)**

   3. *zygote   **(3)**

   endosperm (nucleus)

(iv) Endosperm **or** cotyledon (or seed leaf or embryonic leaf)   **(3)**

Sexual reproduction in the human

In mammals, the male reproductive organs produce haploid (n) motile sperm. These are passed to the female through the penis. Fertilisation is **internal**. It occurs in the **oviduct** of the female when the sperm fuses with the haploid (n) female egg or ovum. The diploid (2n) **zygote** produced divides repeatedly by **mitosis**, finally implanting into the uterus wall. The embryo develops in the uterus for 38 weeks until birth.

Male reproductive system

Testes

- The testes produce haploid sperm in the seminiferous tubules.
- **Diploid cells** known as primary spermatocytes divide by **meiosis** to form haploid sperm cells.
- The sperm are stored in the **epididymis**.
- The testes are enclosed in an external scrotum, which maintains the testes at 2 °C below body temperature. This is essential for sperm production (see fig. 3.54).

Glands

Three glands produce **nourishment** and a **medium** for the sperm to swim in. These are:
- The seminal vesicles
- Cowper's gland
- Prostate gland

Penis

- The penis is used to expel urine during **excretion**.
- It transfers semen during **copulation**.
- The penis is a highly vascular organ that becomes erect due to blood pressure, allowing sexual intercourse.

Testosterone

Testosterone is a hormone produced by the **interstitial cells** in the testes. It stimulates the:

- growth of the testes
- production of sperm cells
- development of secondary sexual characteristics.

Secondary sexual characteristics include:

- The enlargement of the larynx to deepen the voice
- The growth of facial and pubic hair
- Muscular development
- Enlargement of the penis.

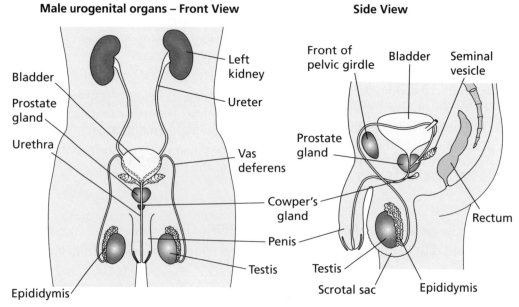

Figure 3.54 Male reproductive system

Female reproductive system

Ovaries

- The ovaries are suspended at the base of the abdominal cavity by ligaments.
- **Haploid eggs** or ova (n) are produced in the **ovaries** when diploid primary oocytes (2n) divide by meiosis (see fig. 3.55).

Fallopian tubes

- Transfer the mature egg from the ovary to the uterus.
- The presence of **cilia** and the secretion of mucus facilitate the movement of the egg cell.
- The lower section of the fallopian tube is known as the **oviduct**. It is here that **fertilisation** will occur.

Uterus

- The uterus (womb) is a thick-walled muscular organ.
- It has an outer layer of muscle with an inner lining known as the **endometrium**.
- The endometrium consists of a mucous membrane with a rich blood supply.

Vagina

- The vagina is a muscular tube linked to the uterus at the cervix.
- The vagina opens to the exterior at the vulva.

Oestrogen

- Oestrogen is one of the female sex hormones produced in the **ovaries**.
- It stimulates the development of the lining of the uterus during the menstrual cycle.

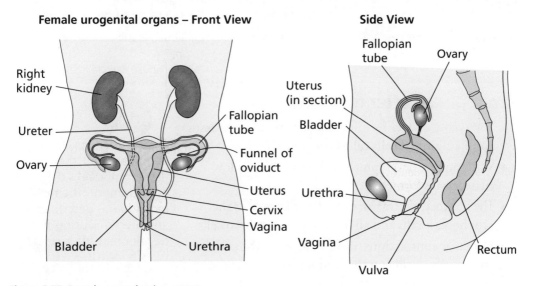

Figure 3.55 Female reproductive system

- It is also responsible for the development of secondary sexual characteristics such as:
  - the development of the breasts
  - widening of the hips
  - lack of facial hair
  - the development of pubic hair.

> **Menstrual Cycle:** 28-day cycle that leads to the preparation of the uterus and the release of an egg from the ovary.
>
> **Menstruation:** The removal from the female body of an unfertilised egg with the built-up lining of the uterus.

Copulation

> **Copulation** involves the insertion of the erect penis into the vagina and the ejaculation of semen.

Birth control

Birth control describes a number of techniques to either plan or avoid conception and pregnancy. Some types are described below.

Type	Method	Principle	(a) Advantages (b) Disadvantages
Natural	Temperature measurement	During ovulation, body temperature increases by 0.5 °C	(a) No side effects (b) There can be many reasons for body temperature variation
Mechanical (barrier)	Condoms	Prevents sperm access to the uterus	(a) Good protection against sexually transmitted diseases (b) Leakages can occur
Chemical	Combined Pill	Doses of oestrogen and progesterone prevent ovulation	(a) Stimulates lighter, more regular periods (b) Can cause nausea
Surgical	Vasectomy	Vas deferens cut and tied	(a) Semen is still produced, without sperm (b) Procedure can be irreversible

Development after fertilisation

- The zygote divides by mitosis a number of times to form a clump of cells called the morula.
- With further development and growth, a hollow blastocyst is formed.
- The blastocyst forms an outer layer known as the trophoblast cells and an inner layer of embryo cells.
- Muscular contractions of the fallopian tube and the movement of cilia on the oviduct wall propel the blastocyst gradually into the uterus.
- The blastocyst obtains nutrition for its cells by active transport of nutrients from the fluids in the fallopian tube (see fig. 3.56).

key point

In humans, for the first eight weeks of development, the new individual is described as an embryo. During further development it is referred to as a foetus.

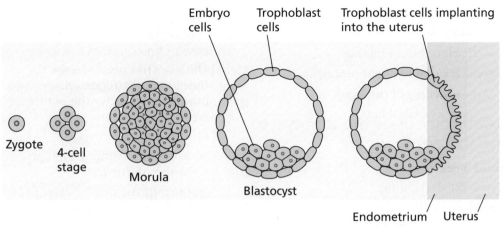

Figure 3.56 Development after fertilisation

Implantation

> **Implantation** is the growth of the fertilised egg into the endometrium, in the uterus, to begin pregnancy.

- After entering the uterus, the trophoblast cells produce tiny extensions that grow into the prepared wall (endometrium) of the uterus.
- The trophoblast cells and the endometrium of the uterus together begin to form the placenta.
- The embryo cells grow and differentiate to form the embryo.
- After implantation, the blastocyst obtains its nutrition by absorption through the trophoblast cells from the endometrium.

Early development of the embryo cells sees the formation of **germ layers**. These give rise to all the tissues and organs of the adult. The three germ layers and the organs and systems they produce are described in the table below.

Germ Layer	Organs and Systems
Ectoderm	Skin, nervous system and sense organs
Mesoderm	Bone, blood vessels and kidneys
Endoderm	Inner lining of intestines and lungs, liver

Placenta

The placenta forms from both the trophoblast cells and the endometrium of the uterus. It is fully formed after twelve weeks of development.

The placenta acts as a link between mother and embryo by:

- transporting food, oxygen and some antibodies from mother to embryo
- transporting carbon dioxide and urea from the embryo to the mother's blood.

The placenta acts as a barrier between mother and embryo by preventing:

- the bloods from mixing
- the transfer of blood proteins
- the transfer of hormones.

Development of the embryo to the thirteenth week

Third week: The brain, spinal cord and nervous system are developing.

Fourth week: Circulation has developed and heartbeat is present. The embryo is 1.5 cm in length. Muscles and **buds** (developing limbs) appear.

The placenta produces the hormones **oestrogen and progesterone** after the eighteenth week of pregnancy.

Both these hormones

- stimulate further development of the uterus wall
- prevent the production of FSH by the pituitary gland.

Eighth week: All organs are developed in miniature. The foetus is now 2.5 cm long.

Thirteenth week: Foetus becomes active. The placenta and amniotic cavity are fully formed. The foetus is 7 cm long and weighs around 30 g (see fig. 3.57).

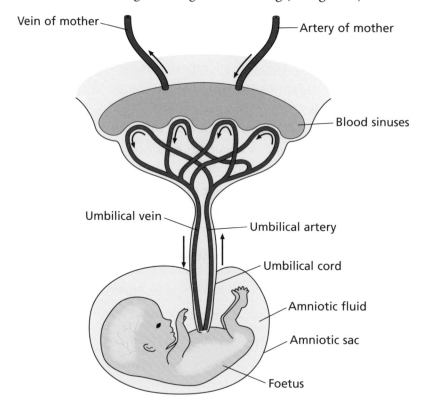

Figure 3.57 Placenta and amniotic sac

Birth (Parturition)

Parturition means giving birth.

- The process begins when the **pituitary** gland produces the hormone **oxytocin**.

- Oxytocin causes the walls of the uterus to begin to contract rhythmically.
- The baby should be upside down with the head at the cervix.
- The amniotic sac ruptures, releasing the amniotic fluid.
- As the contractions continue, the cervix and vagina dilate in preparation for the passage of the baby.
- Further contractions force the head out through the vagina. After a short period, the baby is passed out through the vagina.
- The baby is briefly held upside down to allow the amniotic fluid to drain out from its lungs and air passages so breathing of air can begin.
- The umbilical cord is tied at the navel to prevent excessive blood loss after it is cut.
- Finally, the remaining umbilical cord and the placenta is passed out of the uterus, forming the afterbirth.

Lactation

Lactation is the production of milk in the mother's breasts to feed and protect the newborn baby.

- The process of lactation begins after birth when the **pituitary** gland produces the hormone **prolactin**.
- Prolactin stimulates the mammary glands to begin milk production.

The breast milk produced is very nutritious as it contains:
- large quantities of protein
- antibodies, produced in the mother's body, which will protect the baby from disease.

Infertility

Infertility is a condition, in either sex, which causes conception and pregnancy to be very difficult or impossible.

Male infertility
In males, a low sperm count is a common source of infertility.

Cause
Scientists have observed a distinct decrease in human sperm counts across the population over the last century. Reliable scientific evidence links the accumulation of synthetic organic pollutants in the environment to this observation. Tests have shown that some pesticides are directly linked to sterility in males.

Treatment
Artificial insemination can be used to increase the probability of conception.

Female infertility

Causes

Blockages in the fallopian tubes are a cause of sterility in females. Two common causes are:

- A **functional blockage** such as a mucous plug.
- A **structural blockage** such as scarring.

Treatment

The closer the location of the blockage is to the uterus, the greater the possibility of successful treatment. When the exact nature of the blockage is determined, surgery can be prescribed.

Menstrual disorder

Fibroids (Leiomyomata Uteri)

Description/symptoms

Uterine fibroids are often found in females of reproductive age.

- They are benign (non-cancerous) growths that develop in the muscular wall of the uterus.
- Fibroids can vary in size from tiny to the size of a melon, or larger. Their size and location can result in problems of pain and heavy bleeding.
- Fibroid tumours can reduce fertility and cause difficulties in pregnancy, including miscarriage.

Treatment

There are three main courses of treatment for acute fibroids:

- **Hysterectomy:** This is the complete surgical removal of the uterus and perhaps the ovaries. It is the least preferred option. It is usually used in post-menopausal females when other procedures have failed.
- **Myomectomy:** This is the surgical removal of the fibroids. It is usually reserved for females who wish to preserve fertility.
- **Fibroid embolisation:** This procedure involves the insertion of tiny plastic sponge granules into the artery supplying blood to the fibroid. This restriction of blood flow causes the fibroid to shrink.

In-vitro fertilisation

In-vitro fertilisation is used as a solution to infertility caused by permanent blockage of the oviducts.

- Supplementary FSH and LH may be provided to stimulate multiple egg production in the female.
- The mature female egg cells are then removed from the ovary or fallopian tube.
- The eggs are placed in an in-vitro culturing solution.

- Fertilisation with the male sperm then **occurs outside the body**.
- The developing fertilised eggs are then implanted back into the uterus.

Hormonal control in the menstrual cycle

Hormonal control in the menstrual cycle is a complex process. It is summarised below in order of events as they occur in the cycle (see fig. 3.58).

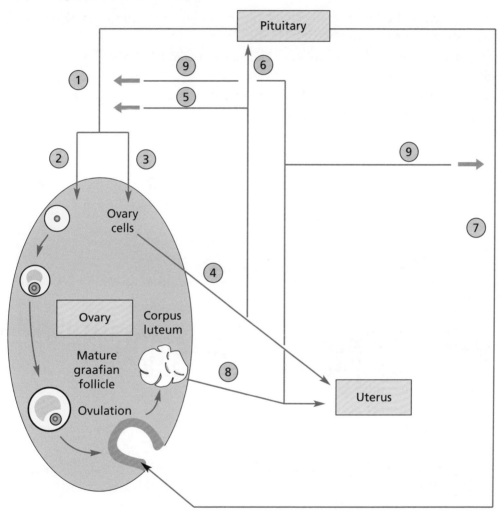

Figure 3.58 Hormonal control in the menstrual cycle

1. The pituitary gland secretes the hormone FSH.
2. FSH stimulates a graafian follicle to mature in the ovary.
3. FSH stimulates cells in the ovary to produce the hormone oestrogen.
4. Oestrogen causes the lining of the uterus to build up.
5. As the concentration of oestrogen rises in the blood, it stops the pituitary producing FSH, thus preventing any more graafian follicles maturing until the cycle is complete.

6. Oestrogen stimulates the pituitary to produce LH.

7. LH causes ovulation, releasing the egg from the ovary. The remaining cells of the graafian follicle form the corpus luteum in the ovary.

8. The corpus luteum produces the hormone progesterone. It causes further build-up of the uterus wall.

9. Progesterone further inhibits the production of FSH by the pituitary. High levels of progesterone in the blood inhibit the production of LH.

When the level of LH drops in the blood, the corpus luteum begins to break down. This causes a drop in the progesterone level in the blood.

A drop in progesterone levels causes the built-up uterus wall to break down, which begins menstruation.

A comparison of the hormone levels, graafian follicle development and the uterus wall during the menstrual cycle is shown in fig. 3.59.

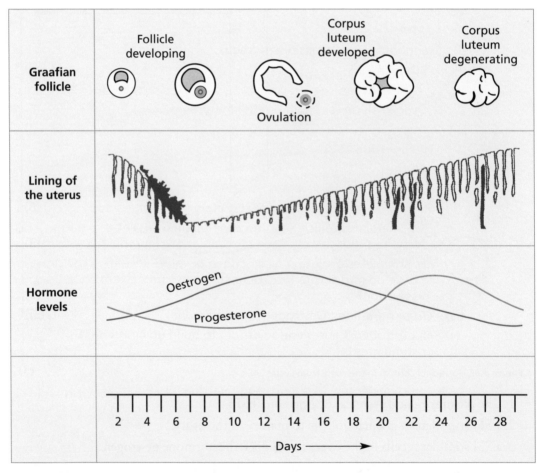

Figure 3.59 Comparison of hormone levels, graafian follicle development and the uterus wall during the menstrual cycle

2016 Q15 (b) HIGHER LEVEL

15. (b) Answer the following questions in relation to the typical human female menstrual cycle.

  (i) State **one** change that occurs, **and** the approximate day(s) of the cycle on which it occurs

    1. in the endometrium.

    2. in the ovary.

  (ii) FHS and LH each plays a role in the cycle. Where in the body are these hormones produced?

  (iii) State **one** role of **each** of these hormones in the cycle.

  (iv) Name **two** other hormones that play a role in the cycle.

  (v) Stating clearly which of the two hormones you have chosen from (iv), give a function in the cycle of that hormone.

LEAVING CERT MARKING SCHEME

15. (b) (i) 1. *Endometrium*: Breaks down (shed)   (Days) 1 – 5

      or   **(3 + 3)**

      Thickens   (Days) 6 – 28

    2. *Ovary*: Follicle (or ovum or egg) matures   (Days) 1 – 14

      or   **(3 + 3)**

      Ovulation   (Days) 13 – 15

      or

      Corpus luteum develops   (Days) 15 – 28

  (ii) *Where FSH and LH produced*: *Pituitary (gland)*   **(3)**

  (iii) *FSH*: Stimulates follicle (egg) to develop (in ovary) **or** stimulates (ovary) to produce oestrogen **or** stimulates LH (production)   **(3)**

    LH: Stimulates ovulation **or** described **or** causes (Graafian follicle) to develop into corpus luteum **or** stimulates progesterone (production)   **(3)**

  (iv) *Other hormones*: Oestrogen / progesterone   **(2[3])**

  (v) *Fn oestrogen*: Causes endometrium to build up or inhibits FSH or stimulates LH

    OR   **(3)**

    Fn progesterone: Maintains endometrium or inhibits LH or inhibits FSH

2015 Q14 (c) HIGHER LEVEL

14. (c) (i) Draw a labelled diagram of the human male reproductive system and its associated glands.

(ii) Put X on the diagram where meiosis occurs.

(iii) Give a function of **one** named gland.

(iv) The diagram shows the structure of a human sperm cell. Part B contains many mitochondria.

1. Suggest why a sperm cell needs so many mitochondria.

2. Mitochondria are inherited exclusively from the mother. Suggest why this is the case.

(v) State the survival times of the egg and sperm in the female body.

LEAVING CERT MARKING SCHEME

14. (c) (i) Diagram: testis + prostate (or seminal vesicles or Cowper's gland) + sperm duct & urethra + penis   **(6, 3, 0)**

Labels: testis, epididymis, sperm duct, seminal vesicle, Cowper's gland, prostate gland, urethra, penis, scrotum   **(3 + 2)**

(ii) X on testes   **(1)**

(iii) Named gland + function   **(3)**

(iv) 1. (Sperm cells) need a lot of energy **or** (sperm cells) need to swim long distances (or described) (compared to their size)   **(3)**

Mitochondria produce energy **or** mitochondria carry out (aerobic) respiration   **(3)**

2. Only the head (of the sperm) enters the egg **or** no sperm mitochondria enter the egg   **(3)**

(v) *Egg*: 12 – 48 hours   **(3)**

Sperm: 0 – 7 days   **(3)**

Glossary

Abiotic Factors   Physical, non-living factors that influence living organisms. Examples: climatic and edaphic factors   12

Absorption   The movement of the products of digestion from the gut into the blood   125

Accommodation   Changing the shape of the lens to focus light onto the retina of the eye   153

ACH (Acetylcholine)   Neurotransmitter carrying impulses in chemical form across a synapse   150

Active (Induced) Immunity   Immunity due to infection or the artificial introduction of a dose of non-disease-causing pathogens, that stimulates antibody production   169

Active Site   A specific, temporary point of attachment on an enzyme, for a substrate   38

Active Transport   The movement of materials across a cell membrane against the diffusion gradient. It requires energy (ATP).   104

Alleles   Different genes that control the same trait and have the same locus on homologous chromosomes   67

Amniotic sac   A membrane, filled with amniotic fluid, surrounding a developing embryo for protection   192

Amoeba   Unicellular animal in pond water. Phylum Protista   104

Anabolic Reaction (Anabolism)   Chemical reaction forming large biomolecules from simple molecules using energy. Example: photosynthesis   49

Antagonistic Muscles   Pairs of voluntary muscles that control the movement of parts of the skeleton. Example: biceps and triceps   167

Antibiotic   Chemical produced by micro-organisms that prevent the growth of, and kill, bacteria   94

Anticodon   Three bases (nucleotides) in tRNA that match a codon on mRNA   79

Antigen   A foreign object (usually a pathogen) that stimulates the production of specific antibodies   169

Appendicular Skeleton   The arms, legs, pectoral girdle and pelvic girdle   164

Artificial Propagation   Procedures used to produce new plants by vegetative propagation (asexual reproduction). Techniques include cutting, grafting, layering and tissue culture (micropropagation).   185

Asepsis   Describes an environment free of contaminating microorganisms   99

Aseptic Technique   A series of steps to prevent contamination of an environment by unwanted micro-organisms   99

Aseptate   Multicellular fungus without dividing cross walls between cells. Example: *Rhizopus*   97

Assimilation   The movement of digested food from the blood into the cells   125

Atherosclerosis   The build up of fatty deposits on arteries. It can cause heart disease if it occurs on the coronary arteries.   117

ATP   High-energy storage molecule. Low energy form is ADP. Made up of adenine (amino acid), ribose (sugar) and phosphates. The energy is stored in the chemical bonds between the phosphates.   50

Autotrophic (Holophytic)   A form of nutrition where an organism makes its own complex materials (biomolecules) from simple molecules using energy. All plants are autotrophic.   93

Auxin   A group of chemicals produced in actively dividing plant tips. They regulate growth (growth regulators).   143

Axon   Long thin section of a neuron that carries impulses away from the cell body   147

Bacteria   A procaryotic 'unicellular' microorganism that exists in every ecosystem on earth   91

Batch Processing   The growth of micro-organisms in a bioprocessor with limited nutrients. On completion all the contents are removed and any useful product must be separated from the mixture.   44

Biceps   Voluntary muscle that raises the lower arm. It is one of an antagonistic pair.   167

Binary Fission   Asexual reproduction involving one parent only. Two cells, genetically identical to the parent, are produced. Meiosis or gametes are not involved in this form of reproduction.   91

Binocular Vision   The combined use of two eyes to provide a 3D image that is accurate in terms of distance and size   154

Biomolecule   A large, complex molecule made up of different elements. Originally produced by plants from simple elements.   5

Bioprocessing   The use of micro-organisms, in industry, to produce large quantities of useful products   44

Bioreactor   A large tank used to culture micro-organisms (or their enzymes) that produce useful products. Factors such as oxygen concentration, pH and temperature are controlled for optimal production.   44

Biosphere   The part of the earth occupied by organisms. It extends from the bottom of the oceans to the upper atmosphere.   11

Biotechnology   Techniques using micro-organisms, or their enzymes, to produce useful products in medicine or industry   44

Biotic Factors   Any factors in an organism's environment that are due to the presence of other organisms. Examples: competition, predation   12

Birth Control   Techniques used to prevent fertilisation and pregnancy during or after copulation   190

Blastocyst Multicellular, hollow structure, formed from the morula, consisting of outer trophoblast and inner embryo layers 190

Blind Spot Point of attachment of the optic nerve to the retina. It is not sensitive to light. 152

Bone Hard tissue made of protein (collagen) and salts (calcium and phosphate) surrounding bone cells (osteoblasts) 163

Bone Marrow Soft tissue located in central parts of long bones. Initially it produces blood cells but later fills with fats to form yellow marrow. 165

Bowman's Capsule Cup-shaped part of a nephron located in the cortex of the kidney. Filtration of blood occurs at this point, producing the glomerular filtrate. 138

Budding Form of asexual reproduction in yeast 185

Cardiac Muscle Specialised heart muscle capable of tireless contraction (systole) and relaxation (diastole) 111

Carnivore An animal that feeds on other animals only. Example: cat, hedgehog 125

Carpel Female reproductive part of flower producing female egg cell. Consists of stigma, style and ovary. 176

Cartilage Flexible tissue containing some protein (collagen). It is present in joints and provides shape in the ear and nose. In joints it provides a smooth surface, to reduce friction and act as a shock absorber. 166

Catabolic Reaction (Catabolism) Chemical reaction breaking down large biomolecules to simple molecules, releasing energy. Example: respiration 56

Cell Body Section of a neuron that contains the nucleus 149

Cell Cycle A sequence of changes a cell goes through between one cell division and the next. It consists of two stages, interphase and mitosis. 63

Central Nervous System The brain and spinal cord 146

Cerebellum Hind portion of the brain that controls muscles and is concerned with balance 146

Cerebrum Largest part of the brain consisting of two cerebral hemispheres which functions in learning and memory 146

Chemical Digestion The use of enzymes to break down large food biomolecules to single units for absorption 127

Chemosynthetic Organism with autotrophic nutrition using the energy from chemical reactions to make biomolecules (food) 94

Chemotropism Growth response of a plant to a chemical stimulus 142

Chitin A carbohydrate found in the cell walls of fungi and in the exoskeleton of insects 96

Choroid Pigmented middle layer of the eye consisting of blood vessels supplying nutrients to the eye 152

Chromosome Threadlike structure in the nucleus, made up of DNA and protein; it contains genes 67

Chromosome Mutation Mutation, due to a change in a chromosome structure or a change in the number of chromosomes present in an organism. Example: Down's syndrome is caused by the presence of an extra chromosome 86

Ciliary Body Muscular layer surrounding the lens in the eye. It changes the shape of the lens for accommodation. 153

Classification The arrangement of different organisms into groups with similar features (often anatomical), for ease of comparison and study 90

Climatic Factors Non-living factors that influence organisms in an ecosystem. Examples: light intensity, temperature 12

Closed Circulatory System Transport system in animals where the blood is enclosed in vessels in a one-way direction of flow 111

Coccus Spherical-shaped bacteria 91

Coding DNA Portion of DNA that makes up a gene. It codes for an enzyme or protein. 81

Codon Three nucleotide bases on mRNA that codes for a specific amino acid 79

Cohesion Theory (Transpiration Pull Theory) Transpiration produces a suction force in the leaves sufficient to draw water from the roots up to the leaves (Theory by Dixon and Joly) 122

Community A naturally occurring group of plant and animal species in an ecosystem 11

Compact Bone Hard tissue made of protein (collagen) and salts (calcium and phosphate) surrounding bone cells (osteoblasts). It forms the rigid outer part of bones that provides mechanical strength. 164

Comparative Anatomy A study of the structural similarities of various organisms used to support the theory of evolution 85

Conjunctiva Thin protective membrane that covers the cornea of the eye 152

Conservation A series of measures to retain viable populations of species in their ecosystems 22

Continuity Process of cells or organisms reproducing to continue living 61

Continuous Flow Processing The growth of micro-organisms in a bioreactor with nutrients continuously being added and the conditions monitored and controlled. Immobilised micro-organisms (or enzymes) allow useful product to be continuously removed without any need for separating procedures. 92

Contractile Vacuole Cell organelle in amoeba used in osmoregulation 104

Control Experiment An experiment identical to the test experiment but without the factor under test being varied 41

Controlled or Fixed Variable Factor in scientific method that is kept constant during experimentation 41

Copulation The passing of semen from the male penis to the vagina of the female during sexual reproduction 188

Cornea Transparent part of the sclera at the front of the eye allowing the entry of light. With the lens it refracts light to form a sharp image on the retina. 152

Corpus Luteum Remains of the graafian follicle in the ovary formed after ovulation. Produces the hormone progesterone. 196

Cotyledon Food store in the seed of non-endospermic plants. Example: broad bean 105

Cowper's Gland Gland in the male reproductive system producing fluid and nutrients for sperm cells 187

Dark Stage Light-independent stage of photosynthesis that occurs in the stroma of the chloroplast. It produces glucose using carbon dioxide, NADPH and ATP. 50

Data A set of values of quantitative or qualitative variables 2

Decline Phase Stage of decrease in micro-organism population, due to lack of nutrients and the build up of wastes 92

Denaturation (Denatured) Deactivation of an enzyme, caused by the permanent changing of the shape of the active site. It can be caused by excessive temperatures or pH changes. 38

Dendrites Branched portions of neuron carrying impulses into the cell body 149

Dermal Tissue Impermeable, protective outer layer of tissue in plants 106

Diastole Relaxation of heart (cardiac) muscle during heart beat 114

Dicotyledon (Dicot) Flowering plant reproducing by seeds with two cotyledons. Example: broad bean 104

Diffusion The movement of a substance from its region of high concentration to a region of low concentration along a diffusion gradient. It can only occur in liquids or gases. 33

Digestion The mechanical and chemical breakdown of food in the body 125

Dihybrid Cross A genetic cross where two characteristics are being observed 67

Diploid An organism with a full complement of two sets of chromosomes (2n) in pairs 61

Discs (vertebral) Discs of cartilage separating vertebrae allowing movement and acting as shock absorbers 166

DNA (Deoxyribonucleic acid) A nucleic acid that makes up genes and chromosomes. It is located in the nucleus and forms a double helix shape. Its base sequence forms the genetic code. 76

DNA Profiling/Fingerprinting Uses the repeating nucleotide sequences in DNA to produce a pattern of bands for the comparison of individuals 81

Dominant The gene that is expressed in the phenotype of the heterozygous condition 67

Dormancy Period where germination does not occur even though factors of oxygen, water and temperature are present. Ensures that germination occurs when conditions are optimal for full development. 188

Dorsal Root Part of spinal nerve entering the spinal cord on the dorsal side. It contains sensory neurons. 147

Double Blind Testing An experimental process in which neither the subjects nor the individuals administering the experiment are aware which procedures are control or test experiments 2

Double Fertilisation Flowering plant fertilisation where two male gametes from pollen fertilise (a) the egg cell forming the zygote (2n); (b) the polar nuclei forming the endosperm (3n) 178

Ecology The scientific study of how organisms interact with each other and their environment 11

Ecosystem A definable area containing a self-sustained community of organisms, interacting with each other and their non-living environment 11

Edaphic Factors Non-living factors in the soil that influence organisms in an ecosystem. Examples: soil pH, soil moisture 12

Egestion The removal of unused, unabsorbed remains of food from the body 125

Embryo Early stage of development of new organism after fertilisation. Formed in the uterus of mammals (190) and in the ovule of plants during sexual reproduction (178).

Embryo Sac Megaspore produced in the ovule of the ovary in the flower. It contains eight haploid nuclei. After fertilisation it develops to form the embryo (2n) and the endosperm (3n). 177

Endocrine Gland Ductless gland that secretes hormones directly into the blood. Examples: testes, ovaries, pituitary, thyroid, adrenal glands 157

Endometrium Tissue rich with blood vessels lining the uterus in preparation for the implantation of a fertilised egg 189

Endoskeleton A skeleton inside an animal, forming a framework, outside of which muscles are attached 163

Endosperm Food store in the seed of an endospermic plant. Example: sunflower 179

Enzyme A protein catalyst produced by organisms 38

Enzyme Saturation An enzyme functioning at its maximum rate under specific conditions. Its rate will not increase if more substrate is added. 38

EPO (Erythropoietin) Hormone produced in the kidneys that stimulates red blood cell production. Used in sport as a hormone supplement. 159

Eukaryotic An organism with cells containing a membrane-bound nucleus and cell organelles 35

Evolution Present-day species have evolved from primitive ancestors, through gradual changes, that occurred over long periods 85

Excretion The removal of the waste products of metabolism from the body 137

Exocrine Gland Gland that secretes substances through a duct. Examples: salivary, pancreatic and sweat glands 157

Experiment A process or procedure used to test a hypothesis 2

Fallopian Tube Tube transporting eggs from the ovary to the uterus 189

Fair Test An experiment that produces good data by only changing one variable in the procedure 2

False Fruit Structure formed after fertilisation usually from some part of the flower other than the carpel. It is used for seed dispersal. 180

Fertilisation The fusion of two haploid gametes to form a diploid zygote 178

Fibrinogen Blood protein involved in clotting wounds 129

Fibroids Benign growths in the uterus that can cause infertility 194

Flower Structure formed by flowering plants for sexual reproduction 176

Food Any substance used by living organisms to provide energy, materials for repair and maintenance or to control metabolism 6

Food Chain Shows a linear feeding relationship between some organisms in an ecosystem 13

Food Web Shows all the feeding relationships in an ecosystem 12

Fossil The remains of a once-living plant or animal 85

Fovea Most light-sensitive part of the retina where light is focused 152

Fruit Structure formed after fertilisation usually from the ovary of the carpel. It is used for seed dispersal. 180

Fungi Family of eukaryotic organisms with cell walls but lacking chlorophyll. Examples: yeast and *Rhizopus.* Cell wall is made of chitin (carbohydrate). Nutrition is either saprophytic or parasitic. 90

Gamete A haploid sex cell capable of fusion 69

Gaseous Exchange The transfer of gases between an organism and its external environment 133

Gene Units of heredity, located on chromosomes in the nucleus. Genes control characteristics or traits and are made of DNA. 69

Gene Mutation A change in the base (nucleotide) sequence of the DNA in a gene which can alter the protein it produces. Example: cystic fibrosis is caused by a gene mutation 86

Genetic Engineering Techniques used to alter the characteristics of an organism by the insertion of a gene into its DNA from another organism. It is often used in the manufacture of large quantities of useful products. 82

Genetic Screening The use of simple diagnostic tests on a large number of individuals to identify those who may have or may pass on a genetic disorder 82

Genetic Testing The use of diagnostic tests to investigate an individual suspected of having a high risk of a genetic disorder based on family history or a positive screening test 82

Genotype The genetic make-up of an organism 69

Geotropism Growth response of a plant to the stimulus of gravity 142

Germination The early stages of growth in a seed to form a new plant. The digestion of food reserves, their translocation to growing tips and respiration, all play a vital role. 180

Glomerular Filtrate A fluid, free of cells and proteins, in the lumen of the nephron. It is produced by the filtration of the blood. 138

Glycolysis The breakdown of glucose to pyruvic acid in respiration. It occurs in the cytoplasm and produces a small amount of energy. Oxygen is not required for this process. 57

Graafian Follicle Cells and fluid-filled cavity surrounding the female egg cell in the ovary. Forms the corpus luteum after ovulation. 159

Ground Tissue Packing tissue in plants with a function of food storage or support 106

Growth Regulator Chemical messenger produced in the growing tips of plants for the purpose of coordination 143

Habitat The part of an ecosystem where individual organisms live 12

Haemoglobin Iron-containing protein in red blood cells that carry oxygen 112

Haemophilia A blood clotting disease caused by a recessive gene on the X chromosome 73

Haploid A cell with half the full complement of chromosomes, which are unpaired 61

Hepatic Portal System The passage of the products of digestion from the intestine to the liver along the hepatic portal vein 111

Herbivore An animal that feeds on plants only. Examples: rabbit, sheep 125

Heredity The passing of traits or characteristics from parents to offspring through genes on chromosomes 67

Heterotrophic A form of nutrition where an organism takes in complex materials (biomolecules) and converts them to small simple molecules, releasing energy. All animals and fungi are heterotrophic. 93

Heterozygous An organism that has two different genes controlling the same trait. Example: Tt 68

Homeostasis The regulation and maintenance of a constant internal environment within an organism 132

Homologous Chromosomes Pairs of chromosomes containing genes that control the same characteristics 62

Homozygous An organism with two identical alleles for a trait or characteristic 68

Hormone A generally slow-acting chemical messenger produced in tiny quantities by an endocrine gland 157

HRT (Hormone Replacement Therapy) Supplementary doses of oestrogen and progesterone used to reduce the effects of menopause. Example: Osteoporosis (thought to increase risk of breast cancer) 159

Hydrogen Bonds Weak, electrostatic bonds that are easily broken and reformed, e.g. (i) bonds between base pairs in DNA; (ii) bonds between water molecules 77

Hydrotropism Growth response of a plant to the stimulus of water 142

Hyperopia (Long sight) blurred vision where light cannot be focused onto the retina when observing near objects. A convex lens is used for correction. 153

Hypothalamus Part of the brain that controls water balance (osmoregulation) and body temperature 147

Hypothesis A testable statement, in scientific method, used to explain an observed event 2

IAA (Indole Acetic Acid) Plant growth regulator produced at growing tips that stimulates cell elongation 143

Immobilised Enzymes Enzymes (or cells), stabilised in a bioprocessor, to produce useful product in continuous flow processing 44

Immunisation Production of immunity (resistance to disease) by artificial means. The administration of vaccines or antibodies provide immunisation. 169

Immunity The ability of the body to resist disease. See Natural and Acquired Immunity 168

Implantation The growth of the fertilised egg into the wall of the uterus to begin pregnancy 191

Incomplete Dominance When neither of a pair of alleles is dominant and both are expressed in the phenotype of the individual. Example: Roan coat colour in cattle 68

Induced Immunity Specific response to the entry of a pathogen into the body involving lymphocytes and antibodies 169

Infertility A condition where fertilisation and pregnancy becomes difficult or impossible 193

Ingestion The taking in of food to the body through the mouth 125

Interneuron Short neuron in the grey matter of the central nervous system that links a sensory neuron directly to a motor neuron in a reflex arc 149

In-vitro fertilisation Process of fertilising eggs with male sperm outside the body for later implantation into the uterus. Often used to promote pregnancy in cases of infertility. 194

Iris Pigmented muscular tissue in front of the lens in the eye. It controls the amount of light entering the eye. 152

Krebs Cycle Second stage of aerobic respiration converting Acetyl CoA to CO_2 and NADH. It occurs in the stroma of the mitochondria. 57

Lactation The production and discharge of milk from the mother's breasts after giving birth 193

Lag Phase Initial stage of slow growth as micro-organisms adapt to a new environment 92

Law or Principle A theory that is confirmed repeatedly by experiment and widely accepted can become a law or principle 2

Lens Flexible transparent structure that focuses light onto the retina 152

Lenticel Openings on the bark of woody plants that allow for gaseous exchange 133

Life (Definition) Anything that has metabolism and the ability to reproduce 5

Ligament A tissue that contains protein (collagen) and joins bones in synovial joints 167

Light Stage Light-dependent stage of photo-synthesis that occurs in the lamellae and grana of the chloroplast. It produces NADPH, ATP and O_2. 50

Linkage Genes controlling different characteristics that are located on the same chromosome are said to be linked. Mendel's Law of Independent Assortment does not hold true for linked genes. 71

Logarithmic Phase Stage of accelerated growth and reproduction by micro-organisms in ideal growing conditions 92

Lymph Colourless liquid in the lymphatic system, formed from the absorption of excess extra-cellular fluid from the tissues 118

Lymph Capillary Absorbs excess extra-cellular fluid from the tissues passing it to lymphatic vessels 118

Lymph Node Swellings on lymphatic vessels that filter foreign particles out of the lymph. Lymph nodes produce lymphocytes and antibodies. 119

Lymphatic Vessel Transports lymph around the body. Valves and lymph nodes are located along its length. 118

Lymphocyte White blood cell in the lymph nodes that protects against disease. It produces specific antibodies against antigens. 169

B Lymphocyte Lymphocytes that mature in the red bone marrow and migrate to the lymph nodes. Most produce specific antibodies in response to an antigen. Some form **memory B cells** to speed up the immune response if infection occurs again. 170

T Lymphocyte Lymphocyte that matures in the thymus gland. Four types Helper T Cells improve the effectiveness of other T cells. Killer T Cells attack unicellular parasites or cells with viruses. **Suppressor T Cells** moderate the immune response. Memory T Cells ensure a rapid response if infection is repeated.   170

Manipulated Variable Factor in scientific method that is changed or varied during the experiment   41

Malt Agar Culture medium for plant fungi (plant yeast on leaves)   101

Mechanical Digestion The physical tearing and crushing of food in the mouth and stomach   127

Medulla Oblongata Part of the brain at the top of the spinal cord involved in involuntary (not conscious) control. It monitors breathing and heart beat rates.   136

Meiosis Cell division where four cells are produced, each with half the number of chromosomes of the parent cell   64

Mendel's First Law (Law of Segregation) The characteristics of organisms are controlled by pairs of alleles which separate at gamete formation. Only one of any pair can enter a gamete.   69

Mendel's Second Law (Law of Independent Assortment) When gametes are formed, each member of a pair of alleles can combine with either member of another pair. This Law does not hold true if genes are linked.   70

Meninges Three membranes that surround the brain and spinal cord containing cerebrospinal fluid   147

Menstrual cycle 28-day cycle that leads to the preparation of the uterus and the release of an egg cell from the ovary   192

Menstruation The removal of an unfertilised egg with the built-up lining of the uterus from the female body   190

Meristematic Tissue (Meristem) Cells actively dividing by mitosis at growing tips in plants.

Apical meristems are located at root and shoot tips.

Lateral meristems form the cambium in vascular bundles and are responsible for secondary thickening (widening of the stem).   106

Metabolism Chemical reactions that occur in organisms   5

Minerals Simple atoms or ions, necessary in small amounts, that must be taken in the diet   8

Mitosis Cell division where two cells are produced each with the same number of chromosomes **or** identical to the parent cell   62

Monera (Prokaryot) Family of organisms that do not have a membrane-bound nucleus or cell organelles (mitochondria or chloroplasts). Example: bacteria   91

Monocotyledon (Monocot) Flowering plant reproducing by seeds with one cotyledon only. Example: grass   105

Monocyte Large white blood cell that protects against disease by engulfing antigens   112

Monohybrid Cross A genetic cross where only one characteristic is being observed   68

Morula Group of undifferentiated cells formed in the oviduct soon after fertilisation   190

Motor Neuron Transfers impulses from the central nervous system to effectors (muscles or glands)   148

mRNA Carries code matching DNA out of the nucleus to a ribosome for translation   79

Mutagen Chemicals or forms of radiation that promote mutations   86

Mutation A change in the base sequence of DNA that alters the genetic code
(See Gene and Chromosome mutations)   86

Myelin Sheath Layer of fatty secretion insulating axons. It speeds up the rate of impulse transmission.   149

Myopia (Short Sight) Blurred vision where light is focused in front of the retina when observing distant objects. A concave lens is used for correction.   153

NADH (Nicotinamide Adenine Dinucleotide) Energy storage molecule. Made up of nicotinamide (from vitamin B), adenine (amino acid) and dinucleotide (two nitrogen-containing bases). A source of energy, hydrogen and electrons for chemical reactions.   50

NADPH (Nicotinamide Adenine Dinucleotide Phosphate) Energy storage molecule. Made up of nicotinamide (from vitamin B), adenine (amino acid), dinucleotide (two nitrogen-containing bases) and phosphate. A source of energy, hydrogen and electrons for chemical reactions.   50

Natural Immunity Non-specific adaptations of the body to prevent the entry and growth of pathogens It can be passive, to prevent the entry, or active, to destroy foreign particles after entry.   168

Natural Selection (Theory of evolution proposed by Darwin and Wallace) The way in which organisms, over time, become better adapted to their environment (due to mutations or genetic changes). Improved characteristics are then passed on to offspring.   85

Nephron Multicellular, tubular structure in the kidney. It functions in excretion, forming urine, and in osmoregulation.   138

Neuron Nerve cell that rapidly transfers impulses by both electrical and chemical means   148

Neurotransmitter Chemical messenger transferring a nerve impulse across a synapse. Examples: acetylcholine (ACH), dopamine   150

Niche Describes the role of an organism in an ecosystem. It shows how and where an organism lives.   12

Nitrogen Cycle The changes that nitrogen and its compounds undergo in nature   19

Nitrogen Fixation The conversion of atmospheric nitrogen (N_2) to nitrates (NO_3^-) or ammonia (NH_3) by bacteria or lightning   20

Non-coding DNA Portion of DNA between genes that does not code for an enzyme or protein   81

Nucleus A membrane-bound structure that contains chromosomes (DNA). It controls the activities of the cell.   31

Nutrient Recycling The reuse and changing in forms of limited quantities of nutrients in nature. Examples: carbon and nitrogen cycles   18

Oestrogen Hormone produced in the ovary that promotes development of:
(a) the uterine wall
(b) secondary sexual characteristics   189

Omnivore An animal that feeds on both plants and animals. Examples: pigs, humans   125

Organ A group of different tissues working together to carry out a function in an organism. Examples: heart, kidney, stomach   65

Organelle A small membrane-bound structure in a eucaryotic cell that has a specific function   31

Organ System A number of organs working together to form a system in the body. Example: the digestive organ system contains the stomach, intestines, pancreas and liver   65

Osmoregulation The control of the salt/water balance in the body   140

Osmosis Movement of water from its region of high concentration to its region of low concentration across a semipermeable membrane   33

Ovary Female reproductive organ producing haploid egg cells (gametes)   189

Oviduct Part of the fallopian tube linking the ovary to the uterus   189

Ovulation The release of a haploid ovum (egg) from the ovary into the fallopian tube   196

Oxyhaemoglobin Oxygenated form of haemoglobin in red blood cells   112

Pacemaker (SA Node) A small mass of specialised muscle cells, in the wall of the right atrium, that initiate heart beat   115

Parasite Organism with heterotrophic nutrition feeding off living organisms causing them harm   17

Passive (Induced) Immunity Immunity, due to introduction of a serum that contains antibodies, from another individual already immune. It can also occur through exchange at the placenta or breast-feeding between mother and offspring.   169

Pathogen Disease-causing microorganism   168

Pentadactyl Limb A five-digit limb common to many four-limbed animals   85

Periosteum Outer layer of connective tissue in bone   165

Peripheral Nervous System All body nerves linked to the central nervous system   146

Peristalsis The movement of food through the alimentary canal by the contractions of circular and longitudinal muscles   127

Perennation The survival of a plant from one growing season to the next by the use of modified roots, stems or buds   123

Petal Flower part used for pollination in insect (animal) pollinated plants   176

Phagocytes (Monocyte) White blood cells that provide immunity. They are produced in the red bone marrow and engulf pathogens.   112

Phenotype Observable characteristics (traits) in an organism, determined by its genes and the genes' interactions with the environment   68

Phloem Transport tissue for food materials (carbohydrate) in plants. Consisting of living, thin-walled, phloem sieve tubes, and companioncells.   107

Phosphorylation The formation of high energy ATP from ADP + P + Energy   50

Photosynthetic Organism with autotrophic nutrition using sunlight to make food   94

Phototropism Growth response of a plant to the stimulus of light. Shoots are positively phototropic, roots are negatively phototropic.   142

Piloerection Involuntary muscular contraction, causing body hairs to rise, creating an insulating layer of air preventing heat loss   152

Pituitary Endocrine gland at the base of the brain that produces a number of hormones   147

Placenta Site of exchange between mother and embryo in the wall of the uterus. Made up of both maternal and embryo tissue it acts as a link and a barrier between the separate blood systems.   191

Plasma The yellowish liquid portion of the blood. It is mainly composed of water with many dissolved substances such as glucose, amino acids, mineral salts and urea.   111

Plasmagel Outer, clear, gel layer of amoeba   104

Plasmasol Inner, fluid layer of amoeba   104

Plasmid A circular loop of DNA in bacteria.It can be replicated and passed easily to other bacteria. It is often used to carry a desirable gene for replication in genetic engineering.   83

Plasmolysis A condition where the cytoplasm pulls away from the cell wall of plant cells, due to water loss. It can lead to wilting.   33

Plumule Structure that develops from the embryo of a seed forming the stem of the new plant   181

Polar nuclei Two haploid nuclei in the embryo sac when fertilised by a male gamete forms the triploid endosperm nucleus giving rise to the endosperm food store   177

Pollen Grains produced in the stamen of the flower containing male gametes. A microspore produced in the anther of the stamen containing a generative and tube nucleus.   176

HL

Pollination Transfer of male pollen to stigma of female carpel. Two types: self and cross pollination. Vectors in cross pollination may be wind or insects. 177

Pollution The release of substances or energy into the environment in large quantities that harm the natural inhabitants 21

Population A group of individuals of the same species in a community 20

Predator Any animal that captures and feeds on another animal 16

Prey An animal that is a source of food for a predator 17

Prokaryot (Monera) Family of organisms that do not have a membrane-bound nucleus or cell organelles (mitochondria or chloroplasts). Example: bacteria 35

Progesterone Hormone produced by the corpus luteum (or the placenta) that promotes the development of the uterine wall 192

Prolactin Hormone produced by the pituitary that stimulates the mammary glands to generate milk 193

Prostate Gland in the male reproductive system producing fluid and nutrients for sperm cells 187

Protista Unicellular, eukaryotic animals. Example: amoeba 104

Pulse A series of dilating waves in arteries, caused by the pressure of blood, pumped from the left ventricle during heart contraction. Pulse can be detected where arteries are close to the skin, e.g. at the wrist. 115

Pupil Opening in the iris that allows light to enter the eye 152

Pyramid of Numbers Represents the numbers of organisms at each trophic level in a food chain 13

Radicle Structure that develops from the embryo of a seed forming the root of the new plant 181

Reabsorption (in the kidney) The movement of useful substances from the glomerular filtrate back into the blood as it flows through the nephron of the kidney 138

Recessive An allele whose expression in phenotype is masked by a dominant allele 69

Red Bone Marrow A soft tissue in the centre of long bones that produces blood cells. Yellow bone marrow forms when red marrow no longer produces blood cells and fills with fats. 165

Reflex Action A very rapid response to a stimulus due to a reflex arc, which does not involve the brain 148

Reflex Arc A simple circuit in the nervous system that provides a very rapid response to a stimulus, without involving the brain 146

Replicates Repeating experiments to gain data to support or refute a hypothesis 2

Retina Inner layer of the eye consisting of light sensitive cells, rods and cones 152

Rhizopus **(Mucor or Bread Mould)** Multicellular, saprophytic fungus, with aseptate hyphae 96

Ribosome Cell organelle made up of RNA and located in the cytoplasm. It is involved in the production of protein (protein synthesis). 31

RNA (Ribonucleic Acid) A nucleic acid in the form of a single helix, mainly found in the cytoplasm 79

rRNA Binds mRNA in place for the process of translation in protein synthesis 79

Saccharomyces **(Yeast)** Unicellular, saprophytic fungus 98

Saprophyte Organism with heterotrophic nutrition feeding off dead organisms 96

Schwann Cell Cell located on the axon of neurons that secretes the myelin sheath 149

Sclera Tough outer protective layer of the eye 152

Secondary Sexual Characteristics Features produced by sex hormones that stimulate changes in the physical characteristics of males and females 188

Seed Reproducing structure of flowering plant formed after fertilisation containing an embryo and a food store (cotyledon or endosperm) 179

Seed dispersal Various methods of spreading seeds to avoid competition. Methods include wind, water, animal and self-dispersal 180

Selectively Permeable Barrier/Semipermeable Membrane A membrane that only allows certain molecules (usually smaller) to pass through. Examples: cell membrane, Visking tubing 33

Sensory Neuron Transfers impulses from receptors to the central nervous system 148

Sepal Outer protective layer of flower bud 176

Sex Chromosomes A pair of chromosomes in mammals that determine the sex of the individual. There are two types, the larger X and the Y chromosome. XX = female XY = male 72

Sex Linked Genes, located on the sex chromosomes, controlling characteristics other than the sex of individual. Example: the recessive genes for haemophila and colour blindness 73

Somatic Cell Any cell in an organism not involved in reproduction 61

Speciation The evolution of one or more species from an existing species. The new groups can no longer interbreed. 85

Species A group of individuals that can interbreed and produce fertile offspring 86

Spinal Nerve Nerve linked to the spinal cord by dorsal and ventral roots 147

Spongy Bone Tissue made of protein (collagen) and salts (calcium and phosphate) surrounding bone cells (osteoblasts). It is located at the ends of long bones. 165

Spore 1. A resting stage of a fungus or bacteria that is capable of resisting adverse conditions 93
2. A haploid structure in flowering plants that produce gametes. Examples: embryo sac and pollen 177

Stamen   Male reproductive part of flower producing pollen. Consists of filament and anther.   176

Stationary Phase   Stage of reduced growth rate in micro-organisms when the population numbers remain static. It occurs due to the lack of nutrients and the build-up of wastes.   92

Sterile/Sterility   An environment free of contaminating micro-organisms   99

Stimulus   Any change in the external or internal environment of an organism that provokes a response in the organism   142

Stoma(ta)   Pores on the underside of leaves that allow for gaseous exchange. (Guard Cells regulate their size.)   123

Substrate   A substance that attaches to an enzyme at its active site. It is converted to product(s) and released.   38

Sweat Gland   Exocrine gland that releases sweat through a duct onto the surface of the skin. It functions in temperature regulation and excretion.   156

Synapse   A minute space between two nerve cells across which chemical messengers (neurotransmitters) are passed   150

Synovial Joint   Freely movable joint in the skeleton. Examples: shoulder, knee and finger joints   166

Systole   Contraction of heart (cardiac) muscle during heartbeat   114

Tendon   A tissue that contains protein (collagen) that attaches muscles to bone to allow movement   167

Testa   Outer impermeable protective coat of seed   179

Testis (Testes)   Male reproductive organ producing haploid sperm cells (gametes)   187

Theory   A hypothesis can become a theory if it is supported by unbiased experiments repeatedly   2

Thigmatropism   Growth response of a plant to the stimulus of touch   142

Tissue   A group of similar cells that have the same functions. Examples: nerve, skin, bone and blood tissues   66

Toxin   A poison released by pathogenic micro-organisms in the body   168

Transcription   The copying of a DNA sequence of nucleotides to mRNA, in the nucleus, during protein synthesis   79

Translation   The conversion of the code on mRNA codons to a sequence of amino acids. It occurs at ribosomes in the cytoplasm, during protein synthesis.   79

Translocation   The transport of nutrients (monosaccharides, amino acids and fatty acids) around a plant. It mainly occurs in the phloem of mature plants.   123

Transpiration   The loss of water vapour from the surface of a plant   122

Transpiration Stream   The flow of liquid water from the roots, up the stem and out to the leaves of a plant   122

Triceps   Voluntary muscle that extends the lower arm. It is one of an antagonistic pair.   167

tRNA   Carries a specific amino acid, matching mRNA, to a ribosome for translation in protein synthesis   79

Trophic Level   The position of an organism in a food chain   13

Tropism   The response of a plant to an external stimulus   142

Turgor/Turgid   A plant cell having absorbed so much water that the vacuole pushes against the cell wall. In this condition no more water can enter the cell.   33

Umbilical cord   Links the placenta to the developing embryo by blood vessels. Carries wastes away from and nutrients to the embryo.   192

Uterus (Womb)   Organ in the abdomen where development of the embryo occurs during reproduction   189

Vaccination   Artificial immunity produced by the introduction of a dose of non-disease-causing pathogens that stimulate antibody production   169

Vaccine   A suspension of weakened or dead pathogens injected into the body to stimulate antibody production. It promotes greater immunity.   169

Variables   Factors in scientific method that can be controlled during experimentation. Examples: temperature, light intensity   3

Vascular tissue   Transport tissue in plants. Examples: xylem and phloem   106

Vasoconstriction   The narrowing of blood vessels to reduce blood flow to the skin. It is caused by involuntary muscular contraction in arterioles, causing an increase in blood pressure. It can be used as a means of retaining body heat.   152

Vegetative propagation   Asexual reproduction in plants. Modified structures such as stem tubers (potato), buds or bulbs (onion) and root tubers (dahlia) give rise to asexual reproduction.   183

Ventral Root   Part of spinal nerve leaving the spinal cord on the ventral side containing motor neurons   147

Vertebral (or intervertebral) Discs   Discs of cartilage separating vertebrae allowing movement and acting as shock absorbers   164

Villus (Villi)   Multiple finger-like projections in the ileum. Richly supplied with blood capillaries and lymph vessels, they increase surface area for absorption.   128

Virus   An obligate parasite consisting of an outer protein coat and either DNA or RNA   171

Visking Tubing   Artificial, semipermeable membrane used in experiments on osmosis   34

Vitamins   Complex biomolecules, necessary in small amounts, that must be taken in the diet   8

Voluntary Muscle   Skeletal muscle under conscious control. Examples: biceps and triceps   167

Waste Management   Measures of disposal, treatment and recycling of wastes to reduce or prevent pollution in the environment   23

Xylem   Transport tissue carrying water and minerals from the roots to the leaves.Thick lignified cells and tracheids.   107

Yeast (*Saccharomyces*)   Unicellular, saprophytic fungus widely used in the baking and brewing industries   98

Zygospore   Thick-walled, resistant, diploid spore produced by *Rhizopus* during sexual reproduction   97

Zygote   Diploid nucleus formed by the fusion of two haploid gametes   178